TEACHER'S PET PUBLICATIONS

PUZZLE PACK
for
Pride and Prejudice

based on the book by
Jane Austen

Written by
William T. Collins

© 2005 Teacher's Pet Publications
All Rights Reserved

The materials in this packet are copyrighted
by Teacher's Pet Publications, Inc.

These pages may be duplicated by the purchaser
for use in the purchaser's own classroom.

Copying any of these materials and distributing them
for any other purpose is a violation of the copyright laws.

© 2005 Teacher's Pet Publications, Inc.
www.tpet.com

INTRODUCTION
If you already own the LitPlan for this title, this Puzzle Pack will refresh your Unit Resource Materials and Vocabulary Resource Materials sections plus give you additional materials you can substitute into the tests. If you do not already have a complete LitPlan, these pages will give you some supplemental materials to use with your own plan. There are two main groups of materials: one set for unit words (such as characters' names, symbols, places, etc.) and one set for vocabulary words associated with the book.

WORD LIST
There is a word list for both the unit words and the vocabulary words. These lists show you which words are being used in the materials and the clues or definitions being used for those words. You may want to give students a word list with clues/definitions to help them, or you may want students to only have a word list (without clues/definitions) if you want them to work a little harder. Both are available for duplication. The word lists can also be your "calling key" for the bingo games.

FILL IN THE BLANK AND MATCHING
There are 4 each of the fill in the blank and matching worksheets for both the unit and vocabulary words. These pages can be used either as extra worksheets for students or as objective parts of a unit test. They can be done individually if students need extra help or as a whole class activity to review the material covered.

MAGIC SQUARES
The magic squares not only reinforce the material covered but also work on reasoning and math skills. Many teachers have told us that their students really enjoy doing these!

WORD SEARCH PUZZLES
The word search words go in all directions, as indicated on your answer keys. Two of the word search puzzles have the clues listed rather than the words. This makes the puzzle a little more difficult, but it reinforces the material better. Two word search puzzles have words only for students who find the clue puzzles too difficult.

CROSSWORD PUZZLES
Both unit and vocabulary word sections have 4 crossword puzzles.

BINGO CARDS
There are 32 individual bingo cards for the unit words and 32 individual bingo cards for the vocabulary words. You can use your word list as a "call list," calling the words at random and marking them off of your list as you go, or you could use the flash cards by cutting them apart and drawing the words at random from a hat (or box or whatever). To make a better review, you might ask for the definition and spelling of each word as you call it out–or you could call out the definitions and have students tell you the words they need to look for on the puzzle.

JUGGLE LETTERS
The vocabulary juggle letter game is intended to help students learn the spellings of the words. One sheet has the definitions listed on it as an extra help for students who need it or to reinforce the definitions if you choose to do so.

FLASH CARDS
We've included a set of vocabulary flash cards you can duplicate, cut, and fold for your students. Some teachers make a few sets for general use by the class; others make a set for each student. Some teachers duplicate them for each student and have the students cut & fold their own. You can cut out just the words and put them in a hat, have each student pick out one word and write the definition and a sentence for that word. Students then swap words and papers, with the next student adding a sentence of his own under the last one. You can have students swap as many times as you like. Each time the student will read the sentences written prior to his own and then add a sentence. You can cut out the words and definitions separately and play "I Have; Who Has?" Each student in the room draws a word and definition. The first student says, "I have (the name of the word). Who has the definition?" The student with the definition reads it then says, "I have (the name of the vocabulary word she has). Who has the definition?" The round continues until all words and definitions have been given.

Pride & Prejudice Word List

No.	Word	Clue/Definition
1.	APPEARANCES	What things seem to be
2.	AUSTEN	Author
3.	BALL	A kind of event where there is dancing
4.	BINGLEY	Rich man of Netherfield
5.	BRIGHTON	Lydia is invited by Col. Forster's wife to go there.
6.	CARRIAGE	Means of transportation
7.	CHARLOTTE	She agrees to marry Mr. Collins although she doesn't love him.
8.	COLLINS	Will inherit Longbourn
9.	DANCE	One does this at a ball.
10.	DARCY	Owner of Pemberley
11.	DEBOURGH	Lady Catherine ___
12.	DINE	Eat dinner
13.	ELIZABETH	Frank and independent Bennet daughter
14.	EYES	Elizabeth's attracted Darcy
15.	FITZWILLIAM	Darcy's pleasant cousin; colonel
16.	GARDEN	A beautiful place to stroll and take walks
17.	GARDINER	She warns Elizabeth not to fall in love with Wickham.
18.	GEORGIANA	Darcy's sister
19.	HELP	Darcy ___ed the Bennets; aided
20.	JANE	Eldest Bennet daughter
21.	JEALOUS	Miss Bingley is ___ that Elizabeth has Darcy's interest.
22.	KITTY	Younger sister under Lydia's influence
23.	LETTERS	Means of communication
24.	LONDON	Town where Lydia and Wickham went
25.	LYDIA	Elopes with Wickham
26.	MARRIAGE	Mr. Collins disregards Elizabeth's rejection of his ___ proposal.
27.	MONEY	Darcy had lots of it; he was rich.
28.	MUD	Elizabeth arrived at Netherfield covered in it.
29.	NETHERFIELD	Mrs. Bennet wants Eliz. & Jane to stay overnight at ___ Hall.
30.	NOTE	Short letter
31.	PAY	Darcy had to ___ Wickham's debts.
32.	PREJUDICE	Pride and ___
33.	PRIDE	___ and Prejudice
34.	REPUTATION	The Bennets were concerned about Lydia's ___.
35.	ROSINGS	Lady Catherine's home
36.	WICKHAM	Military man; gambler
37.	WORLD	The more I see of the ___ the more I am dissatisfied with it.

Copyrighted

Pride & Prejudice Fill In The Blanks 1

_____

1. Will inherit Longbourn
2. Mrs. Bennet wants Eliz. & Jane to stay overnight at ___ Hall.
3. Darcy ___ed the Bennets; aided
4. Short letter
5. She warns Elizabeth not to fall in love with Wickham.
6. Darcy had lots of it; he was rich.
7. Lady Catherine's home
8. Military man; gambler
9. Mr. Collins disregards Elizabeth's rejection of his ___ proposal.
10. Darcy's pleasant cousin; colonel
11. Means of communication
12. The Bennets were concerned about Lydia's ___.
13. Eldest Bennet daughter
14. A beautiful place to stroll and take walks
15. Owner of Pemberley
16. Town where Lydia and Wickham went
17. Frank and independent Bennet daughter
18. Elizabeth arrived at Netherfield covered in it.
19. Miss Bingley is ___ that Elizabeth has Darcy's interest.
20. Elizabeth's attracted Darcy

Pride & Prejudice Fill In The Blanks 1 Answer Key

COLLINS	1. Will inherit Longbourn
NETHERFIELD	2. Mrs. Bennet wants Eliz. & Jane to stay overnight at ___ Hall.
HELP	3. Darcy ___ed the Bennets; aided
NOTE	4. Short letter
GARDINER	5. She warns Elizabeth not to fall in love with Wickham.
MONEY	6. Darcy had lots of it; he was rich.
ROSINGS	7. Lady Catherine's home
WICKHAM	8. Military man; gambler
MARRIAGE	9. Mr. Collins disregards Elizabeth's rejection of his ___ proposal.
FITZWILLIAM	10. Darcy's pleasant cousin; colonel
LETTERS	11. Means of communication
REPUTATION	12. The Bennets were concerned about Lydia's ___.
JANE	13. Eldest Bennet daughter
GARDEN	14. A beautiful place to stroll and take walks
DARCY	15. Owner of Pemberley
LONDON	16. Town where Lydia and Wickham went
ELIZABETH	17. Frank and independent Bennet daughter
MUD	18. Elizabeth arrived at Netherfield covered in it.
JEALOUS	19. Miss Bingley is ___ that Elizabeth has Darcy's interest.
EYES	20. Elizabeth's attracted Darcy

Pride & Prejudice Fill In The Blanks 2

_____ 1. Lady Catherine ___

_____ 2. Lady Catherine's home

_____ 3. Rich man of Netherfield

_____ 4. Military man; gambler

_____ 5. Short letter

_____ 6. Lydia is invited by Col. Forster's wife to go there.

_____ 7. Author

_____ 8. Means of transportation

_____ 9. Darcy's pleasant cousin; colonel

_____ 10. Miss Bingley is ___ that Elizabeth has Darcy's interest.

_____ 11. The Bennets were concerned about Lydia's ___.

_____ 12. The more I see of the __ the more I am dissatisfied with it.

_____ 13. Town where Lydia and Wickham went

_____ 14. A beautiful place to stroll and take walks

_____ 15. Frank and independent Bennet daughter

_____ 16. She warns Elizabeth not to fall in love with Wickham.

_____ 17. Eat dinner

_____ 18. Darcy had to ___ Wickham's debts.

_____ 19. Mr. Collins disregards Elizabeth's rejection of his ___ proposal.

_____ 20. Owner of Pemberley

Pride & Prejudice Fill In The Blanks 2 Answer Key

Answer	Clue
DEBOURGH	1. Lady Catherine ___
ROSINGS	2. Lady Catherine's home
BINGLEY	3. Rich man of Netherfield
WICKHAM	4. Military man; gambler
NOTE	5. Short letter
BRIGHTON	6. Lydia is invited by Col. Forster's wife to go there.
AUSTEN	7. Author
CARRIAGE	8. Means of transportation
FITZWILLIAM	9. Darcy's pleasant cousin; colonel
JEALOUS	10. Miss Bingley is ___ that Elizabeth has Darcy's interest.
REPUTATION	11. The Bennets were concerned about Lydia's ___.
WORLD	12. The more I see of the __ the more I am dissatisfied with it.
LONDON	13. Town where Lydia and Wickham went
GARDEN	14. A beautiful place to stroll and take walks
ELIZABETH	15. Frank and independent Bennet daughter
GARDINER	16. She warns Elizabeth not to fall in love with Wickham.
DINE	17. Eat dinner
PAY	18. Darcy had to ___ Wickham's debts.
MARRIAGE	19. Mr. Collins disregards Elizabeth's rejection of his ___ proposal.
DARCY	20. Owner of Pemberley

Pride & Prejudice Fill In The Blanks 3

_____   1. A beautiful place to stroll and take walks

_____   2. Lady Catherine ___

_____   3. Younger sister under Lydia's influence

_____   4. Town where Lydia and Wickham went

_____   5. Lady Catherine's home

_____   6. Rich man of Netherfield

_____   7. Eldest Bennet daughter

_____   8. Elizabeth arrived at Netherfield covered in it.

_____   9. Author

_____   10. Owner of Pemberley

_____   11. Means of transportation

_____   12. Miss Bingley is ___ that Elizabeth has Darcy's interest.

_____   13. What things seem to be

_____   14. The Bennets were concerned about Lydia's ___.

_____   15. Elizabeth's attracted Darcy

_____   16. She warns Elizabeth not to fall in love with Wickham.

_____   17. Darcy's sister

_____   18. Frank and independent Bennet daughter

_____   19. One does this at a ball.

_____   20. Lydia is invited by Col. Forster's wife to go there.

Pride & Prejudice Fill In The Blanks 3 Answer Key

GARDEN	1. A beautiful place to stroll and take walks
DEBOURGH	2. Lady Catherine ___
KITTY	3. Younger sister under Lydia's influence
LONDON	4. Town where Lydia and Wickham went
ROSINGS	5. Lady Catherine's home
BINGLEY	6. Rich man of Netherfield
JANE	7. Eldest Bennet daughter
MUD	8. Elizabeth arrived at Netherfield covered in it.
AUSTEN	9. Author
DARCY	10. Owner of Pemberley
CARRIAGE	11. Means of transportation
JEALOUS	12. Miss Bingley is ___ that Elizabeth has Darcy's interest.
APPEARANCES	13. What things seem to be
REPUTATION	14. The Bennets were concerned about Lydia's ___.
EYES	15. Elizabeth's attracted Darcy
GARDINER	16. She warns Elizabeth not to fall in love with Wickham.
GEORGIANA	17. Darcy's sister
ELIZABETH	18. Frank and independent Bennet daughter
DANCE	19. One does this at a ball.
BRIGHTON	20. Lydia is invited by Col. Forster's wife to go there.

Copyrighted

Pride & Prejudice Fill In The Blanks 4

_____

1. She agrees to marry Mr. Collins although she doesn't love him.
2. Frank and independent Bennet daughter
3. What things seem to be
4. Darcy had lots of it; he was rich.
5. Military man; gambler
6. Lady Catherine ___
7. Means of transportation
8. Eldest Bennet daughter
9. Owner of Pemberley
10. Darcy's sister
11. Short letter
12. A beautiful place to stroll and take walks
13. Eat dinner
14. Elizabeth's attracted Darcy
15. She warns Elizabeth not to fall in love with Wickham.
16. Means of communication
17. One does this at a ball.
18. ___ and Prejudice
19. Darcy had to ___ Wickham's debts.
20. Rich man of Netherfield

Pride & Prejudice Fill In The Blanks 4 Answer Key

CHARLOTTE	1. She agrees to marry Mr. Collins although she doesn't love him.
ELIZABETH	2. Frank and independent Bennet daughter
APPEARANCES	3. What things seem to be
MONEY	4. Darcy had lots of it; he was rich.
WICKHAM	5. Military man; gambler
DEBOURGH	6. Lady Catherine ___
CARRIAGE	7. Means of transportation
JANE	8. Eldest Bennet daughter
DARCY	9. Owner of Pemberley
GEORGIANA	10. Darcy's sister
NOTE	11. Short letter
GARDEN	12. A beautiful place to stroll and take walks
DINE	13. Eat dinner
EYES	14. Elizabeth's attracted Darcy
GARDINER	15. She warns Elizabeth not to fall in love with Wickham.
LETTERS	16. Means of communication
DANCE	17. One does this at a ball.
PRIDE	18. ___ and Prejudice
PAY	19. Darcy had to ___ Wickham's debts.
BINGLEY	20. Rich man of Netherfield

Pride & Prejudice Matching 1

___ 1. LONDON	A. Elopes with Wickham
___ 2. ELIZABETH	B. A beautiful place to stroll and take walks
___ 3. FITZWILLIAM	C. Eat dinner
___ 4. JANE	D. Eldest Bennet daughter
___ 5. ROSINGS	E. Owner of Pemberley
___ 6. DEBOURGH	F. What things seem to be
___ 7. PREJUDICE	G. Town where Lydia and Wickham went
___ 8. APPEARANCES	H. Lady Catherine's home
___ 9. CARRIAGE	I. Pride and ___
___ 10. GARDEN	J. Lady Catherine ___
___ 11. MUD	K. The more I see of the ___ the more I am dissatisfied with it.
___ 12. BALL	L. Military man; gambler
___ 13. JEALOUS	M. She agrees to marry Mr. Collins although she doesn't love him.
___ 14. GEORGIANA	N. Author
___ 15. KITTY	O. Miss Bingley is ___ that Elizabeth has Darcy's interest.
___ 16. NOTE	P. Darcy had to ___ Wickham's debts.
___ 17. LYDIA	Q. Darcy's pleasant cousin; colonel
___ 18. DINE	R. Younger sister under Lydia's influence
___ 19. DARCY	S. A kind of event where there is dancing
___ 20. WORLD	T. Means of transportation
___ 21. WICKHAM	U. Short letter
___ 22. CHARLOTTE	V. Elizabeth arrived at Netherfield covered in it.
___ 23. PAY	W. Darcy's sister
___ 24. NETHERFIELD	X. Frank and independent Bennet daughter
___ 25. AUSTEN	Y. Mrs. Bennet wants Eliz. & Jane to stay overnight at ___ Hall.

Pride & Prejudice Matching 1 Answer Key

G - 1. LONDON	A.	Elopes with Wickham
X - 2. ELIZABETH	B.	A beautiful place to stroll and take walks
Q - 3. FITZWILLIAM	C.	Eat dinner
D - 4. JANE	D.	Eldest Bennet daughter
H - 5. ROSINGS	E.	Owner of Pemberley
J - 6. DEBOURGH	F.	What things seem to be
I - 7. PREJUDICE	G.	Town where Lydia and Wickham went
F - 8. APPEARANCES	H.	Lady Catherine's home
T - 9. CARRIAGE	I.	Pride and ___
B - 10. GARDEN	J.	Lady Catherine ___
V - 11. MUD	K.	The more I see of the ___ the more I am dissatisfied with it.
S - 12. BALL	L.	Military man; gambler
O - 13. JEALOUS	M.	She agrees to marry Mr. Collins although she doesn't love him.
W - 14. GEORGIANA	N.	Author
R - 15. KITTY	O.	Miss Bingley is ___ that Elizabeth has Darcy's interest.
U - 16. NOTE	P.	Darcy had to ___ Wickham's debts.
A - 17. LYDIA	Q.	Darcy's pleasant cousin; colonel
C - 18. DINE	R.	Younger sister under Lydia's influence
E - 19. DARCY	S.	A kind of event where there is dancing
K - 20. WORLD	T.	Means of transportation
L - 21. WICKHAM	U.	Short letter
M - 22. CHARLOTTE	V.	Elizabeth arrived at Netherfield covered in it.
P - 23. PAY	W.	Darcy's sister
Y - 24. NETHERFIELD	X.	Frank and independent Bennet daughter
N - 25. AUSTEN	Y.	Mrs. Bennet wants Eliz. & Jane to stay overnight at ___ Hall.

Copyrighted

Pride & Prejudice Matching 2

___ 1. LETTERS
___ 2. BINGLEY
___ 3. WICKHAM
___ 4. DARCY
___ 5. NOTE
___ 6. REPUTATION
___ 7. KITTY
___ 8. HELP
___ 9. GARDEN
___ 10. PAY
___ 11. MONEY
___ 12. JANE
___ 13. ELIZABETH
___ 14. NETHERFIELD
___ 15. FITZWILLIAM
___ 16. COLLINS
___ 17. CARRIAGE
___ 18. MARRIAGE
___ 19. PRIDE
___ 20. APPEARANCES
___ 21. EYES
___ 22. LYDIA
___ 23. MUD
___ 24. GEORGIANA
___ 25. GARDINER

A. Darcy had lots of it; he was rich.
B. The Bennets were concerned about Lydia's ___.
C. Darcy's sister
D. Elopes with Wickham
E. Mr. Collins disregards Elizabeth's rejection of his ___ proposal.
F. A beautiful place to stroll and take walks
G. She warns Elizabeth not to fall in love with Wickham.
H. ___ and Prejudice
I. Owner of Pemberley
J. Younger sister under Lydia's influence
K. Elizabeth's attracted Darcy
L. Rich man of Netherfield
M. Short letter
N. Frank and independent Bennet daughter
O. Darcy's pleasant cousin; colonel
P. Darcy ___ed the Bennets; aided
Q. Elizabeth arrived at Netherfield covered in it.
R. Mrs. Bennet wants Eliz. & Jane to stay overnight at ___ Hall.
S. What things seem to be
T. Military man; gambler
U. Means of transportation
V. Means of communication
W. Will inherit Longbourn
X. Darcy had to ___ Wickham's debts.
Y. Eldest Bennet daughter

Pride & Prejudice Matching 2 Answer Key

V - 1.	LETTERS	A.	Darcy had lots of it; he was rich.
L - 2.	BINGLEY	B.	The Bennets were concerned about Lydia's ___.
T - 3.	WICKHAM	C.	Darcy's sister
I - 4.	DARCY	D.	Elopes with Wickham
M - 5.	NOTE	E.	Mr. Collins disregards Elizabeth's rejection of his ___ proposal.
B - 6.	REPUTATION	F.	A beautiful place to stroll and take walks
J - 7.	KITTY	G.	She warns Elizabeth not to fall in love with Wickham.
P - 8.	HELP	H.	___ and Prejudice
F - 9.	GARDEN	I.	Owner of Pemberley
X - 10.	PAY	J.	Younger sister under Lydia's influence
A - 11.	MONEY	K.	Elizabeth's attracted Darcy
Y - 12.	JANE	L.	Rich man of Netherfield
N - 13.	ELIZABETH	M.	Short letter
R - 14.	NETHERFIELD	N.	Frank and independent Bennet daughter
O - 15.	FITZWILLIAM	O.	Darcy's pleasant cousin; colonel
W - 16.	COLLINS	P.	Darcy ___ed the Bennets; aided
U - 17.	CARRIAGE	Q.	Elizabeth arrived at Netherfield covered in it.
E - 18.	MARRIAGE	R.	Mrs. Bennet wants Eliz. & Jane to stay overnight at ___ Hall.
H - 19.	PRIDE	S.	What things seem to be
S - 20.	APPEARANCES	T.	Military man; gambler
K - 21.	EYES	U.	Means of transportation
D - 22.	LYDIA	V.	Means of communication
Q - 23.	MUD	W.	Will inherit Longbourn
C - 24.	GEORGIANA	X.	Darcy had to ___ Wickham's debts.
G - 25.	GARDINER	Y.	Eldest Bennet daughter

Pride & Prejudice Matching 3

___ 1. ELIZABETH
___ 2. REPUTATION
___ 3. ROSINGS
___ 4. GARDINER
___ 5. NOTE
___ 6. CARRIAGE
___ 7. BALL
___ 8. FITZWILLIAM
___ 9. COLLINS
___ 10. GEORGIANA
___ 11. GARDEN
___ 12. HELP
___ 13. JANE
___ 14. APPEARANCES
___ 15. MONEY
___ 16. MUD
___ 17. PREJUDICE
___ 18. BRIGHTON
___ 19. MARRIAGE
___ 20. EYES
___ 21. JEALOUS
___ 22. CHARLOTTE
___ 23. KITTY
___ 24. DINE
___ 25. PAY

A. Darcy ___ed the Bennets; aided
B. Darcy's pleasant cousin; colonel
C. Darcy had to ___ Wickham's debts.
D. A beautiful place to stroll and take walks
E. A kind of event where there is dancing
F. Elizabeth's attracted Darcy
G. Younger sister under Lydia's influence
H. Lady Catherine's home
I. What things seem to be
J. She warns Elizabeth not to fall in love with Wickham.
K. Short letter
L. Pride and ___
M. Eat dinner
N. Mr. Collins disregards Elizabeth's rejection of his ___ proposal.
O. Lydia is invited by Col. Forster's wife to go there.
P. Means of transportation
Q. Will inherit Longbourn
R. Eldest Bennet daughter
S. Darcy's sister
T. Darcy had lots of it; he was rich.
U. Miss Bingley is ___ that Elizabeth has Darcy's interest.
V. Frank and independent Bennet daughter
W. The Bennets were concerned about Lydia's ___.
X. Elizabeth arrived at Netherfield covered in it.
Y. She agrees to marry Mr. Collins although she doesn't love him.

Pride & Prejudice Matching 3 Answer Key

V - 1. ELIZABETH		A. Darcy ___ed the Bennets; aided
W - 2. REPUTATION		B. Darcy's pleasant cousin; colonel
H - 3. ROSINGS		C. Darcy had to ___ Wickham's debts.
J - 4. GARDINER		D. A beautiful place to stroll and take walks
K - 5. NOTE		E. A kind of event where there is dancing
P - 6. CARRIAGE		F. Elizabeth's attracted Darcy
E - 7. BALL		G. Younger sister under Lydia's influence
B - 8. FITZWILLIAM		H. Lady Catherine's home
Q - 9. COLLINS		I. What things seem to be
S - 10. GEORGIANA		J. She warns Elizabeth not to fall in love with Wickham.
D - 11. GARDEN		K. Short letter
A - 12. HELP		L. Pride and ___
R - 13. JANE		M. Eat dinner
I - 14. APPEARANCES		N. Mr. Collins disregards Elizabeth's rejection of his ___ proposal.
T - 15. MONEY		O. Lydia is invited by Col. Forster's wife to go there.
X - 16. MUD		P. Means of transportation
L - 17. PREJUDICE		Q. Will inherit Longbourn
O - 18. BRIGHTON		R. Eldest Bennet daughter
N - 19. MARRIAGE		S. Darcy's sister
F - 20. EYES		T. Darcy had lots of it; he was rich.
U - 21. JEALOUS		U. Miss Bingley is ___ that Elizabeth has Darcy's interest.
Y - 22. CHARLOTTE		V. Frank and independent Bennet daughter
G - 23. KITTY		W. The Bennets were concerned about Lydia's ___.
M - 24. DINE		X. Elizabeth arrived at Netherfield covered in it.
C - 25. PAY		Y. She agrees to marry Mr. Collins although she doesn't love him.

Pride & Prejudice Matching 4

___ 1. EYES   A. Means of transportation
___ 2. FITZWILLIAM   B. She agrees to marry Mr. Collins although she doesn't love him.
___ 3. HELP   C. Darcy had to ___ Wickham's debts.
___ 4. DANCE   D. Owner of Pemberley
___ 5. REPUTATION   E. Darcy's pleasant cousin; colonel
___ 6. LONDON   F. Darcy's sister
___ 7. APPEARANCES   G. Short letter
___ 8. WORLD   H. What things seem to be
___ 9. JEALOUS   I. Author
___ 10. JANE   J. Eldest Bennet daughter
___ 11. PRIDE   K. Elizabeth's attracted Darcy
___ 12. ELIZABETH   L. Town where Lydia and Wickham went
___ 13. NOTE   M. Darcy had lots of it; he was rich.
___ 14. LYDIA   N. Darcy ___ed the Bennets; aided
___ 15. GEORGIANA   O. Pride and ___
___ 16. LETTERS   P. Frank and independent Bennet daughter
___ 17. MONEY   Q. ___ and Prejudice
___ 18. CARRIAGE   R. Means of communication
___ 19. DARCY   S. Elopes with Wickham
___ 20. NETHERFIELD   T. Miss Bingley is ___ that Elizabeth has Darcy's interest.
___ 21. BRIGHTON   U. Lydia is invited by Col. Forster's wife to go there.
___ 22. PAY   V. The more I see of the __ the more I am dissatisfied with it.
___ 23. PREJUDICE   W. The Bennets were concerned about Lydia's ___.
___ 24. AUSTEN   X. One does this at a ball.
___ 25. CHARLOTTE   Y. Mrs. Bennet wants Eliz. & Jane to stay overnight at ___ Hall.

Pride & Prejudice Matching 4 Answer Key

K - 1.	EYES	A.	Means of transportation
E - 2.	FITZWILLIAM	B.	She agrees to marry Mr. Collins although she doesn't love him.
N - 3.	HELP	C.	Darcy had to ___ Wickham's debts.
X - 4.	DANCE	D.	Owner of Pemberley
W - 5.	REPUTATION	E.	Darcy's pleasant cousin; colonel
L - 6.	LONDON	F.	Darcy's sister
H - 7.	APPEARANCES	G.	Short letter
V - 8.	WORLD	H.	What things seem to be
T - 9.	JEALOUS	I.	Author
J - 10.	JANE	J.	Eldest Bennet daughter
Q - 11.	PRIDE	K.	Elizabeth's attracted Darcy
P - 12.	ELIZABETH	L.	Town where Lydia and Wickham went
G - 13.	NOTE	M.	Darcy had lots of it; he was rich.
S - 14.	LYDIA	N.	Darcy ___ed the Bennets; aided
F - 15.	GEORGIANA	O.	Pride and ___
R - 16.	LETTERS	P.	Frank and independent Bennet daughter
M - 17.	MONEY	Q.	___ and Prejudice
A - 18.	CARRIAGE	R.	Means of communication
D - 19.	DARCY	S.	Elopes with Wickham
Y - 20.	NETHERFIELD	T.	Miss Bingley is ___ that Elizabeth has Darcy's interest.
U - 21.	BRIGHTON	U.	Lydia is invited by Col. Forster's wife to go there.
C - 22.	PAY	V.	The more I see of the __ the more I am dissatisfied with it.
O - 23.	PREJUDICE	W.	The Bennets were concerned about Lydia's ___.
I - 24.	AUSTEN	X.	One does this at a ball.
B - 25.	CHARLOTTE	Y.	Mrs. Bennet wants Eliz. & Jane to stay overnight at ___ Hall.

Pride & Prejudice Magic Squares 1

Match the definition with the vocabulary word. Put your answers in the magic squares below. When your answers are correct, all columns and rows will add to the same number.

A. COLLINS   E. EYES   I. GEORGIANA   M. WICKHAM
B. PAY   F. LONDON   J. KITTY   N. ELIZABETH
C. AUSTEN   G. DANCE   K. FITZWILLIAM   O. MARRIAGE
D. BALL   H. GARDEN   L. CHARLOTTE   P. JANE

1. Town where Lydia and Wickham went
2. Darcy's sister
3. Mr. Collins disregards Elizabeth's rejection of his ___ proposal.
4. A kind of event where there is dancing
5. Military man; gambler
6. Darcy had to ___ Wickham's debts.
7. A beautiful place to stroll and take walks
8. Darcy's pleasant cousin; colonel
9. Author
10. Eldest Bennet daughter
11. Younger sister under Lydia's influence
12. Elizabeth's attracted Darcy
13. She agrees to marry Mr. Collins although she doesn't love him.
14. One does this at a ball.
15. Will inherit Longbourn
16. Frank and independent Bennet daughter

A= 15	B= 6	C= 9	D= 4
E= 12	F= 1	G= 14	H= 7
I= 2	J= 11	K= 8	L= 13
M= 5	N= 16	O= 3	P= 10

Pride & Prejudice Magic Squares 1 Answer Key

Match the definition with the vocabulary word. Put your answers in the magic squares below. When your answers are correct, all columns and rows will add to the same number.

A. COLLINS
B. PAY
C. AUSTEN
D. BALL
E. EYES
F. LONDON
G. DANCE
H. GARDEN
I. GEORGIANA
J. KITTY
K. FITZWILLIAM
L. CHARLOTTE
M. WICKHAM
N. ELIZABETH
O. MARRIAGE
P. JANE

1. Town where Lydia and Wickham went
2. Darcy's sister
3. Mr. Collins disregards Elizabeth's rejection of his ___ proposal.
4. A kind of event where there is dancing
5. Military man; gambler
6. Darcy had to ___ Wickham's debts.
7. A beautiful place to stroll and take walks
8. Darcy's pleasant cousin; colonel
9. Author
10. Eldest Bennet daughter
11. Younger sister under Lydia's influence
12. Elizabeth's attracted Darcy
13. She agrees to marry Mr. Collins although she doesn't love him.
14. One does this at a ball.
15. Will inherit Longbourn
16. Frank and independent Bennet daughter

A=15	B=6	C=9	D=4
E=12	F=1	G=14	H=7
I=2	J=11	K=8	L=13
M=5	N=16	O=3	P=10

Copyrighted

Pride & Prejudice Magic Squares 2

Match the definition with the vocabulary word. Put your answers in the magic squares below. When your answers are correct, all columns and rows will add to the same number.

A. CARRIAGE
B. NOTE
C. GARDEN
D. KITTY
E. LONDON
F. MARRIAGE
G. HELP
H. COLLINS
I. WICKHAM
J. DINE
K. MONEY
L. FITZWILLIAM
M. JEALOUS
N. LETTERS
O. REPUTATION
P. ELIZABETH

1. The Bennets were concerned about Lydia's ___.
2. Eat dinner
3. Will inherit Longbourn
4. Means of transportation
5. Younger sister under Lydia's influence
6. Town where Lydia and Wickham went
7. Darcy had lots of it; he was rich.
8. Means of communication
9. Mr. Collins disregards Elizabeth's rejection of his ___ proposal.
10. A beautiful place to stroll and take walks
11. Miss Bingley is ___ that Elizabeth has Darcy's interest.
12. Darcy's pleasant cousin; colonel
13. Military man; gambler
14. Frank and independent Bennet daughter
15. Short letter
16. Darcy ___ed the Bennets; aided

A=	B=	C=	D=
E=	F=	G=	H=
I=	J=	K=	L=
M=	N=	O=	P=

Pride & Prejudice Magic Squares 2 Answer Key

Match the definition with the vocabulary word. Put your answers in the magic squares below. When your answers are correct, all columns and rows will add to the same number.

A. CARRIAGE
B. NOTE
C. GARDEN
D. KITTY
E. LONDON
F. MARRIAGE
G. HELP
H. COLLINS
I. WICKHAM
J. DINE
K. MONEY
L. FITZWILLIAM
M. JEALOUS
N. LETTERS
O. REPUTATION
P. ELIZABETH

1. The Bennets were concerned about Lydia's ___.
2. Eat dinner
3. Will inherit Longbourn
4. Means of transportation
5. Younger sister under Lydia's influence
6. Town where Lydia and Wickham went
7. Darcy had lots of it; he was rich.
8. Means of communication
9. Mr. Collins disregards Elizabeth's rejection of his ___ proposal.
10. A beautiful place to stroll and take walks
11. Miss Bingley is ___ that Elizabeth has Darcy's interest.
12. Darcy's pleasant cousin; colonel
13. Military man; gambler
14. Frank and independent Bennet daughter
15. Short letter
16. Darcy ___ed the Bennets; aided

A=4	B=15	C=10	D=5
E=6	F=9	G=16	H=3
I=13	J=2	K=7	L=12
M=11	N=8	O=1	P=14

Pride & Prejudice Magic Squares 3

Match the definition with the vocabulary word. Put your answers in the magic squares below. When your answers are correct, all columns and rows will add to the same number.

A. MARRIAGE
B. DEBOURGH
C. GARDINER
D. HELP
E. ELIZABETH
F. FITZWILLIAM
G. EYES
H. AUSTEN
I. BALL
J. KITTY
K. LETTERS
L. GARDEN
M. JANE
N. ROSINGS
O. LONDON
P. MONEY

1. Author
2. Eldest Bennet daughter
3. Lady Catherine ___
4. Means of communication
5. Younger sister under Lydia's influence
6. She warns Elizabeth not to fall in love with Wickham.
7. Darcy had lots of it; he was rich.
8. Frank and independent Bennet daughter
9. Town where Lydia and Wickham went
10. Darcy's pleasant cousin; colonel
11. A kind of event where there is dancing
12. Darcy ___ed the Bennets; aided
13. Mr. Collins disregards Elizabeth's rejection of his ___ proposal.
14. A beautiful place to stroll and take walks
15. Elizabeth's attracted Darcy
16. Lady Catherine's home

A=	B=	C=	D=
E=	F=	G=	H=
I=	J=	K=	L=
M=	N=	O=	P=

Pride & Prejudice Magic Squares 3 Answer Key

Match the definition with the vocabulary word. Put your answers in the magic squares below. When your answers are correct, all columns and rows will add to the same number.

A. MARRIAGE
B. DEBOURGH
C. GARDINER
D. HELP
E. ELIZABETH
F. FITZWILLIAM
G. EYES
H. AUSTEN
I. BALL
J. KITTY
K. LETTERS
L. GARDEN
M. JANE
N. ROSINGS
O. LONDON
P. MONEY

1. Author
2. Eldest Bennet daughter
3. Lady Catherine ___
4. Means of communication
5. Younger sister under Lydia's influence
6. She warns Elizabeth not to fall in love with Wickham.
7. Darcy had lots of it; he was rich.
8. Frank and independent Bennet daughter
9. Town where Lydia and Wickham went
10. Darcy's pleasant cousin; colonel
11. A kind of event where there is dancing
12. Darcy ___ed the Bennets; aided
13. Mr. Collins disregards Elizabeth's rejection of his ___ proposal.
14. A beautiful place to stroll and take walks
15. Elizabeth's attracted Darcy
16. Lady Catherine's home

A=13	B=3	C=6	D=12
E=8	F=10	G=15	H=1
I=11	J=5	K=4	L=14
M=2	N=16	O=9	P=7

Pride & Prejudice Magic Squares 4

Match the definition with the vocabulary word. Put your answers in the magic squares below. When your answers are correct, all columns and rows will add to the same number.

A. ELIZABETH
B. LETTERS
C. DEBOURGH
D. MARRIAGE
E. DANCE
F. GARDEN
G. LYDIA
H. WORLD
I. NETHERFIELD
J. PAY
K. BALL
L. APPEARANCES
M. CHARLOTTE
N. CARRIAGE
O. JEALOUS
P. BINGLEY

1. Miss Bingley is ___ that Elizabeth has Darcy's interest.
2. Mr. Collins disregards Elizabeth's rejection of his ___ proposal.
3. Darcy had to ___ Wickham's debts.
4. One does this at a ball.
5. Mrs. Bennet wants Eliz. & Jane to stay overnight at ___ Hall.
6. A beautiful place to stroll and take walks
7. Rich man of Netherfield
8. Lady Catherine ___
9. The more I see of the __ the more I am dissatisfied with it.
10. A kind of event where there is dancing
11. Frank and independent Bennet daughter
12. Means of transportation
13. Means of communication
14. She agrees to marry Mr. Collins although she doesn't love him.
15. Elopes with Wickham
16. What things seem to be

A=	B=	C=	D=
E=	F=	G=	H=
I=	J=	K=	L=
M=	N=	O=	P=

Pride & Prejudice Magic Squares 4 Answer Key

Match the definition with the vocabulary word. Put your answers in the magic squares below. When your answers are correct, all columns and rows will add to the same number.

A. ELIZABETH   E. DANCE   I. NETHERFIELD   M. CHARLOTTE
B. LETTERS   F. GARDEN   J. PAY   N. CARRIAGE
C. DEBOURGH   G. LYDIA   K. BALL   O. JEALOUS
D. MARRIAGE   H. WORLD   L. APPEARANCES   P. BINGLEY

1. Miss Bingley is ___ that Elizabeth has Darcy's interest.
2. Mr. Collins disregards Elizabeth's rejection of his ___ proposal.
3. Darcy had to ___ Wickham's debts.
4. One does this at a ball.
5. Mrs. Bennet wants Eliz. & Jane to stay overnight at ___ Hall.
6. A beautiful place to stroll and take walks
7. Rich man of Netherfield
8. Lady Catherine ___
9. The more I see of the ___ the more I am dissatisfied with it.
10. A kind of event where there is dancing
11. Frank and independent Bennet daughter
12. Means of transportation
13. Means of communication
14. She agrees to marry Mr. Collins although she doesn't love him.
15. Elopes with Wickham
16. What things seem to be

A=11	B=13	C=8	D=2
E=4	F=6	G=15	H=9
I=5	J=3	K=10	L=16
M=14	N=12	O=1	P=7

Pride & Prejudice Word Search 1

Words are placed backwards, forward, diagonally, up and down. Clues listed below can help you find the words. Circle the hidden vocabulary words in the maze.

```
P T F D E Y E S N E T H E R F I E L D T
P B I Y L N M G J F H G H J Y R C Q Q W
Y F T W M O D X K B X M L T V C J Z B X
N F Z N Q I Z C H D K J L M W M X B V J
V L W R M T Y V S E D C X O P T L R Y T
J X I N W A Y R V B Y C G Y N Q C O Z X
T B L K V T G P B O D G H N B D Z S J B
L X L Q F U X L D U Y Z R T K J O I E K
M K I Y A P P E A R A N C E S D A N C E
D D A D R E N W E G H C O J R H A G S F
F I M I W R G N Y H Z M L M E J W S Z M
X N D T N X I Z B R C O L F T V W P A C
G E G A R D E N E T O N I N T D A R C Y
H W F G R G E T G Z L E N X E T R E J T
J S O A T M T L A J Y Y S M L I N J E D
K W G R C O U T I B D G L L A O A U A S
B I B A L L P D R Z I H L G T B U D L H
V C T R R D T X R F A N E H S L S I O Y
S K A T C R B V A Z C B G H M P T C U R
N H N C Y M J P C T R I E L H Q E E S F
C A N A I G R O E G R P N T E S N J J Z
S M J S F Q W M K B H E L P H Y J Z J P
```

A beautiful place to stroll and take walks (6)
A kind of event where there is dancing (4)
Author (6)
Darcy ___ed the Bennets; aided (4)
Darcy had lots of it; he was rich. (5)
Darcy had to ___ Wickham's debts. (3)
Darcy's pleasant cousin; colonel (11)
Darcy's sister (9)
Eat dinner (4)
Eldest Bennet daughter (4)
Elizabeth arrived at Netherfield covered in it. (3)
Elizabeth's attracted Darcy (4)
Elopes with Wickham (5)
Frank and independent Bennet daughter (9)
Lady Catherine ___ (8)
Lady Catherine's home (7)
Lydia is invited by Col. Forster's wife to go there. (8)
Means of communication (7)
Means of transportation (8)
Military man; gambler (7)
Miss Bingley is ___ that Elizabeth has Darcy's interest. (7)

Mr. Collins disregards Elizabeth's rejection of his ___ proposal. (8)
Mrs. Bennet wants Eliz. & Jane to stay overnight at ___ Hall. (11)
One does this at a ball. (5)
Owner of Pemberley (5)
Pride and ___ (9)
Rich man of Netherfield (7)
She agrees to marry Mr. Collins although she doesn't love him. (9)
She warns Elizabeth not to fall in love with Wickham. (8)
Short letter (4)
The Bennets were concerned about Lydia's ___. (10)
The more I see of the __ the more I am dissatisfied with it. (5)
Town where Lydia and Wickham went (6)
What things seem to be (11)
Will inherit Longbourn (7)
Younger sister under Lydia's influence (5)
___ and Prejudice (5)

Pride & Prejudice Word Search 1 Answer Key

Words are placed backwards, forward, diagonally, up and down. Clues listed below can help you find the words. Circle the hidden vocabulary words in the maze.

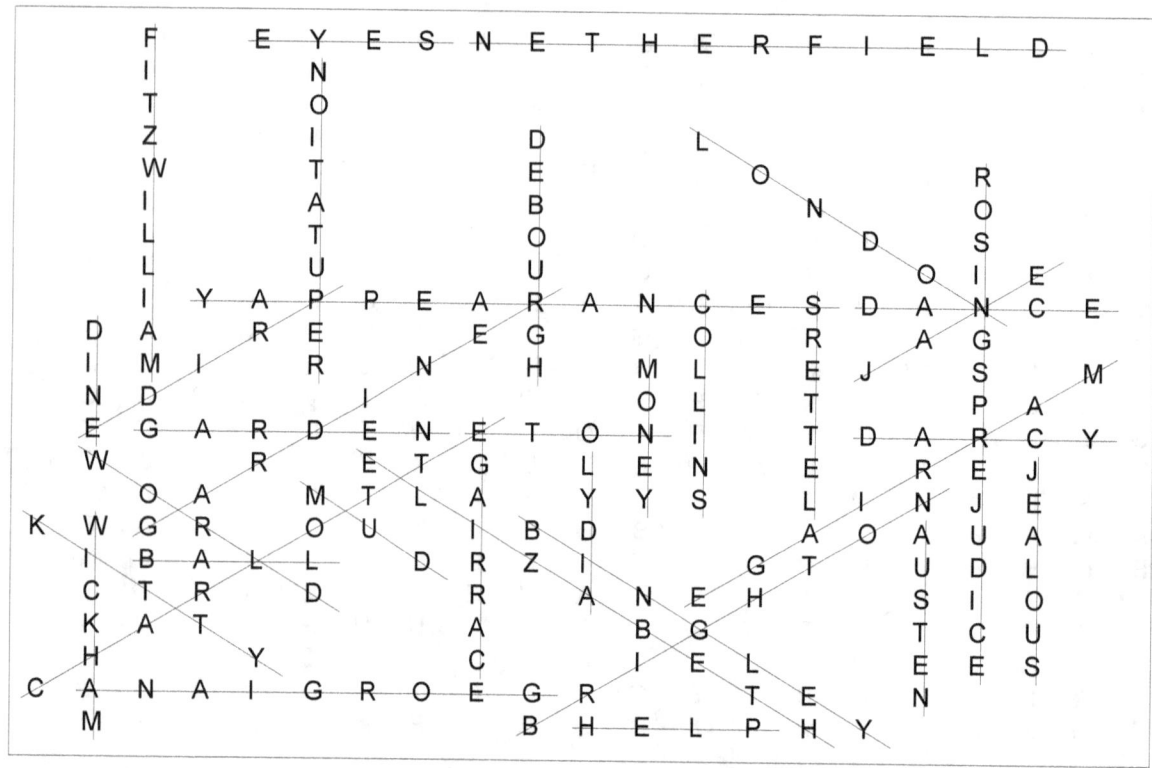

A beautiful place to stroll and take walks (6)
A kind of event where there is dancing (4)
Author (6)
Darcy ___ed the Bennets; aided (4)
Darcy had lots of it; he was rich. (5)
Darcy had to ___ Wickham's debts. (3)
Darcy's pleasant cousin; colonel (11)
Darcy's sister (9)
Eat dinner (4)
Eldest Bennet daughter (4)
Elizabeth arrived at Netherfield covered in it. (3)
Elizabeth's attracted Darcy (4)
Elopes with Wickham (5)
Frank and independent Bennet daughter (9)
Lady Catherine ___ (8)
Lady Catherine's home (7)
Lydia is invited by Col. Forster's wife to go there. (8)
Means of communication (7)
Means of transportation (8)
Military man; gambler (7)
Miss Bingley is ___ that Elizabeth has Darcy's interest. (7)

Mr. Collins disregards Elizabeth's rejection of his ___ proposal. (8)
Mrs. Bennet wants Eliz. & Jane to stay overnight at ___ Hall. (11)
One does this at a ball. (5)
Owner of Pemberley (5)
Pride and ___ (9)
Rich man of Netherfield (7)
She agrees to marry Mr. Collins although she doesn't love him. (9)
She warns Elizabeth not to fall in love with Wickham. (8)
Short letter (4)
The Bennets were concerned about Lydia's ___. (10)
The more I see of the ___ the more I am dissatisfied with it. (5)
Town where Lydia and Wickham went (6)
What things seem to be (11)
Will inherit Longbourn (7)
Younger sister under Lydia's influence (5)
___ and Prejudice (5)

30
Copyrighted

Pride & Prejudice Word Search 2

Words are placed backwards, forward, diagonally, up and down. Clues listed below can help you find the words. Circle the hidden vocabulary words in the maze.

```
G E O R G I A N A V M T V H M A Y M L K
V C Z W R W C D M A S N T F T P Y U V M
F I Y W V S Y W H Y T E Q L Q P N D R S
I D C R C Y Q K B L B T X X H E O C Q D
T U H F L J C B X A Z H Z Y T A I E B J
Z J Z Q R I G R Z N X E F H Q R T G C B
W E M T W P J I X O K R T J K A A A L J
I R X G C S L K T T R F G Q Q N T I F P
L P C H A E K D S H F I M L L C U R T K
L M F L S R P I S G F E O J Z E P R S Z
I Q K T P F D N H I B L N F E S E A S V
A K K D A N C E P R I D E R D A R C Y D
M X H W Y J L N N B E G Y L O E L T Y C
W B R N S P Z A Z B A P R G N S T O Q W
N Q S X P S Z J O I L O J I C I I J U F
L E T T E R S U R B W Y D K K T N N S S
P K J H H Q R R N W I R V D N O F N G G
R J V S F G A E M N A N K L D S I K N S
K R E S H M T V N G B D G N Y L B J J Y
J Y V R Z S Y B G O W A O L L D R Z J M
E Y X W U C T D C T T L L O E N I X X B
D C H A R L O T T E Y E C L B Y W A H N
```

A beautiful place to stroll and take walks (6)
A kind of event where there is dancing (4)
Author (6)
Darcy ___ed the Bennets; aided (4)
Darcy had lots of it; he was rich. (5)
Darcy had to ___ Wickham's debts. (3)
Darcy's pleasant cousin; colonel (11)
Darcy's sister (9)
Eat dinner (4)
Eldest Bennet daughter (4)
Elizabeth arrived at Netherfield covered in it. (3)
Elizabeth's attracted Darcy (4)
Elopes with Wickham (5)
Frank and independent Bennet daughter (9)
Lady Catherine ___ (8)
Lady Catherine's home (7)
Lydia is invited by Col. Forster's wife to go there. (8)
Means of communication (7)
Means of transportation (8)
Military man; gambler (7)
Miss Bingley is ___ that Elizabeth has Darcy's interest. (7)

Mr. Collins disregards Elizabeth's rejection of his ___ proposal. (8)
Mrs. Bennet wants Eliz. & Jane to stay overnight at ___ Hall. (11)
One does this at a ball. (5)
Owner of Pemberley (5)
Pride and ___ (9)
Rich man of Netherfield (7)
She agrees to marry Mr. Collins although she doesn't love him. (9)
She warns Elizabeth not to fall in love with Wickham. (8)
Short letter (4)
The Bennets were concerned about Lydia's ___. (10)
The more I see of the __ the more I am dissatisfied with it. (5)
Town where Lydia and Wickham went (6)
What things seem to be (11)
Will inherit Longbourn (7)
Younger sister under Lydia's influence (5)
___ and Prejudice (5)

Pride & Prejudice Word Search 2 Answer Key

Words are placed backwards, forward, diagonally, up and down. Clues listed below can help you find the words. Circle the hidden vocabulary words in the maze.

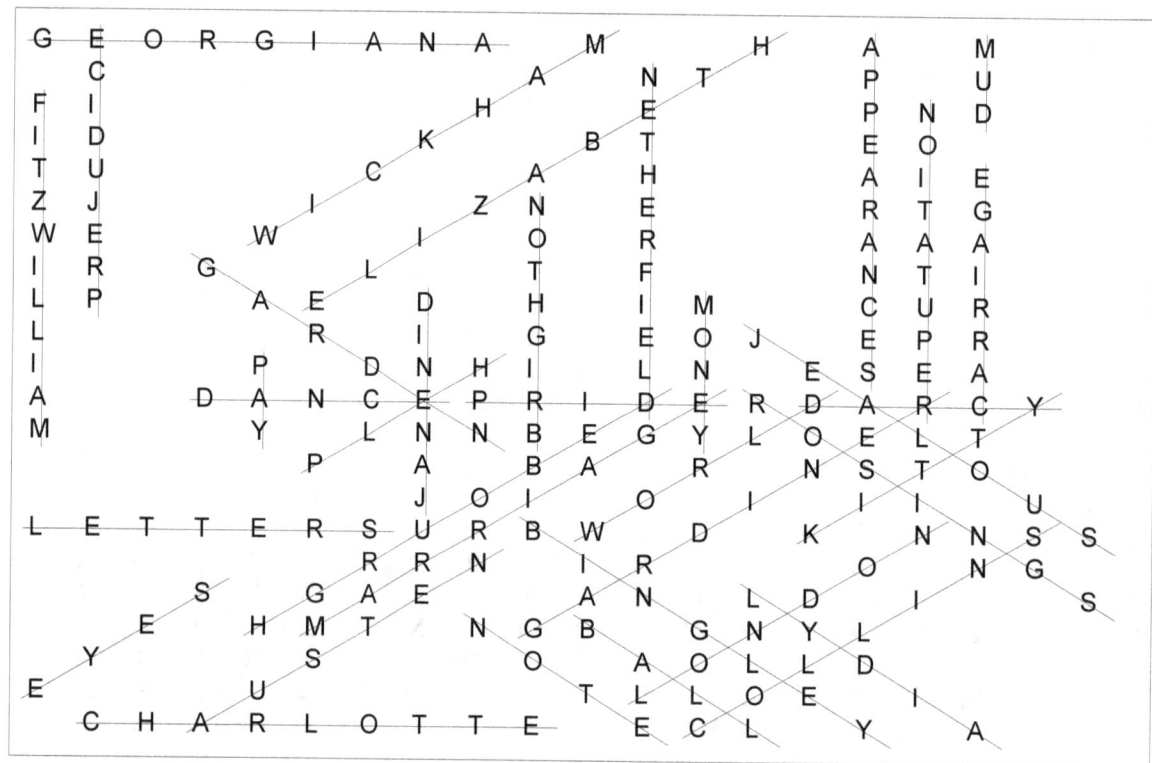

A beautiful place to stroll and take walks (6)
A kind of event where there is dancing (4)
Author (6)
Darcy ___ed the Bennets; aided (4)
Darcy had lots of it; he was rich. (5)
Darcy had to ___ Wickham's debts. (3)
Darcy's pleasant cousin; colonel (11)
Darcy's sister (9)
Eat dinner (4)
Eldest Bennet daughter (4)
Elizabeth arrived at Netherfield covered in it. (3)
Elizabeth's attracted Darcy (4)
Elopes with Wickham (5)
Frank and independent Bennet daughter (9)
Lady Catherine ___ (8)
Lady Catherine's home (7)
Lydia is invited by Col. Forster's wife to go there. (8)
Means of communication (7)
Means of transportation (8)
Military man; gambler (7)
Miss Bingley is ___ that Elizabeth has Darcy's interest. (7)

Mr. Collins disregards Elizabeth's rejection of his ___ proposal. (8)
Mrs. Bennet wants Eliz. & Jane to stay overnight at ___ Hall. (11)
One does this at a ball. (5)
Owner of Pemberley (5)
Pride and ___ (9)
Rich man of Netherfield (7)
She agrees to marry Mr. Collins although she doesn't love him. (9)
She warns Elizabeth not to fall in love with Wickham. (8)
Short letter (4)
The Bennets were concerned about Lydia's ___. (10)
The more I see of the __ the more I am dissatisfied with it. (5)
Town where Lydia and Wickham went (6)
What things seem to be (11)
Will inherit Longbourn (7)
Younger sister under Lydia's influence (5)
___ and Prejudice (5)

Pride & Prejudice Word Search 3

Words are placed backwards, forward, diagonally, up and down. Words listed below are included in the maze. Circle the hidden vocabulary words in the maze.

```
G R E P U T A T I O N D E B O U R G H V
S A J B Q D J H Q S E G A I R R A M P Q
F Z R N B K B N K B J H L N Z S V J R T
Z I W D R K L R D G W T H G Z J G K K P
Z S T G E O R G I A N A K L W D R E Q F
F R J Z Y N D H H G P T Z E D O C Y C C
L O D T W K C W H R H R Z Y K N R J O P
Q S T G J I I S B V H T V S A E K L K Z
T I P B H C L G Y A S T O D G L L F D Q
K N S F K N S L W R L P D N W I E M V R
W G V H S F E R I F T L V Z N Z C H V M
C S A I D Y L T C A H S J S N A I B G G
S M P D Q Y C L H J M W F S S B D J S B
K Q P C G D J T O E M C L R G E U G X P
R N E C M R A T Z N R G B E D T J A D W
B B A C Q S J R N Q D F Y T R H E R I T
X K R N J U D N C F E O I T N R D N F
C H A R L O T T E Y M O N E Y A P I E G
X P N N T L Z S E W Q B T L L R N J Q
X F C O J A L S N D S S C N E D I E P Q
C Z E T V E J A N E U X N H G R D R M D
H Y S E W J B E G A I R R A C F E M U D
```

APPEARANCES   DANCE   GARDINER   LYDIA   PRIDE

AUSTEN   DARCY   GEORGIANA   MARRIAGE   REPUTATION

BALL   DEBOURGH   HELP   MONEY   ROSINGS

BINGLEY   DINE   JANE   MUD   WICKHAM

BRIGHTON   ELIZABETH   JEALOUS   NETHERFIELD   WORLD

CARRIAGE   EYES   KITTY   NOTE

CHARLOTTE   FITZWILLIAM   LETTERS   PAY

COLLINS   GARDEN   LONDON   PREJUDICE

Pride & Prejudice Word Search 3 Answer Key

Words are placed backwards, forward, diagonally, up and down. Words listed below are included in the maze. Circle the hidden vocabulary words in the maze.

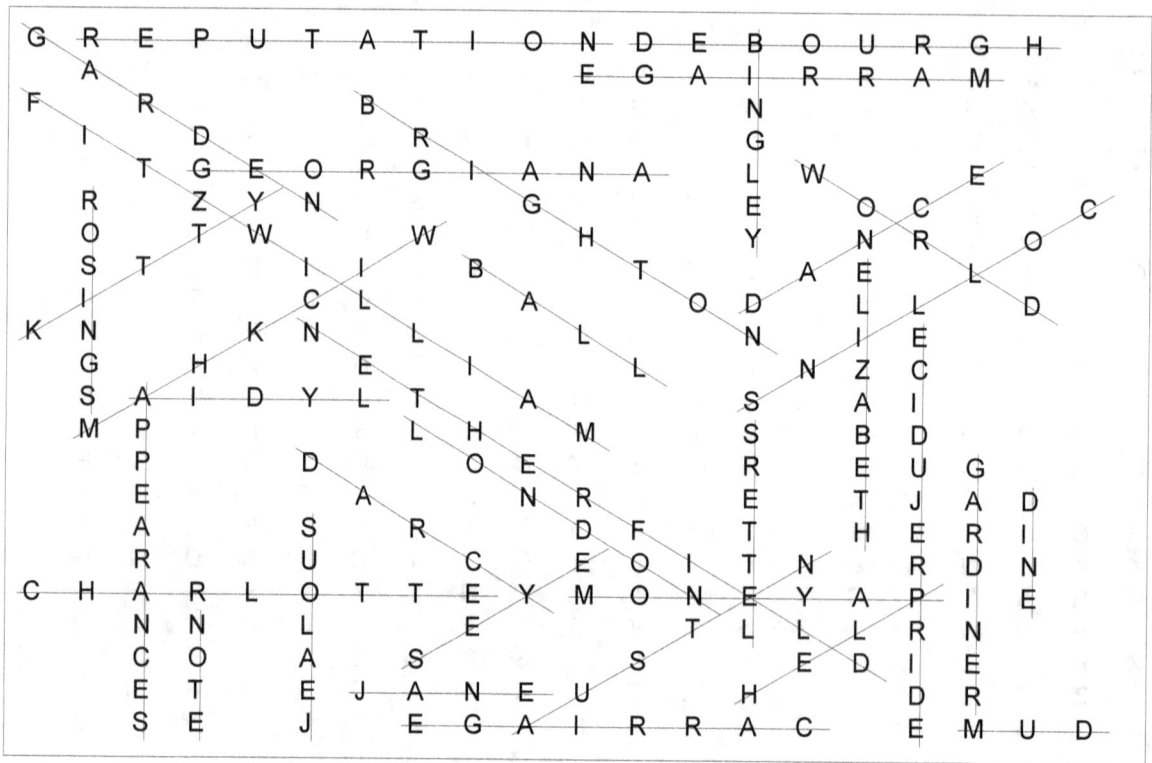

APPEARANCES	DANCE	GARDINER	LYDIA	PRIDE
AUSTEN	DARCY	GEORGIANA	MARRIAGE	REPUTATION
BALL	DEBOURGH	HELP	MONEY	ROSINGS
BINGLEY	DINE	JANE	MUD	WICKHAM
BRIGHTON	ELIZABETH	JEALOUS	NETHERFIELD	WORLD
CARRIAGE	EYES	KITTY	NOTE	
CHARLOTTE	FITZWILLIAM	LETTERS	PAY	
COLLINS	GARDEN	LONDON	PREJUDICE	

Pride & Prejudice Word Search 4

Words are placed backwards, forward, diagonally, up and down. Words listed below are included in the maze. Circle the hidden vocabulary words in the maze.

```
F I T Z W I L L I A M D A R C Y N A B L
M R S T S L G C B Y C P O E W D E P I F
N F N Y N F S R M H V S M P O T T P N Q
B R I G H T O N A B I N M U R Z H E G X
M T L W Y X Q N N O A Q T L V E A L V
M F L P V P A K G D H R Q A D H R R E F
T F O Z B I K S N K W Y X T J S F A Y Z
V M C B G W Q O C X N R D I E K I N Z N
B R S R F F L I Y T F P L O A N E C G Y
N K O P M M W X V Y T R Q N L B L E M T
J E D V Q A C R B P X E G Q O Y D S M F
G R R C Y H R G R L F J B L U V M Z P S
L W K H H R E R X B W U E T S R P F K Z
M Y M M P V G V I R Z D L J V M R J I V
R E N I D R A G P A B I I L Y P I Z T L
W T A P X G I B Q K G C Z K Y D D F T E
L C I C H A R L O T T E A U S T E N Y F
S P D V D R R F J V T Y B Q K N Q E E T
C D Y B A D A B Y O R V E A I R S M N X
H E L P N E C E N A J Y T D L M Z U O M
Z H D T C N B F R M A X H K C L C D M B
L E T T E R S K Y P D E B O U R G H P P
```

APPEARANCES	DANCE	GARDINER	LYDIA	PRIDE
AUSTEN	DARCY	GEORGIANA	MARRIAGE	REPUTATION
BALL	DEBOURGH	HELP	MONEY	ROSINGS
BINGLEY	DINE	JANE	MUD	WICKHAM
BRIGHTON	ELIZABETH	JEALOUS	NETHERFIELD	WORLD
CARRIAGE	EYES	KITTY	NOTE	
CHARLOTTE	FITZWILLIAM	LETTERS	PAY	
COLLINS	GARDEN	LONDON	PREJUDICE	

Pride & Prejudice Word Search 4 Answer Key

Words are placed backwards, forward, diagonally, up and down. Words listed below are included in the maze. Circle the hidden vocabulary words in the maze.

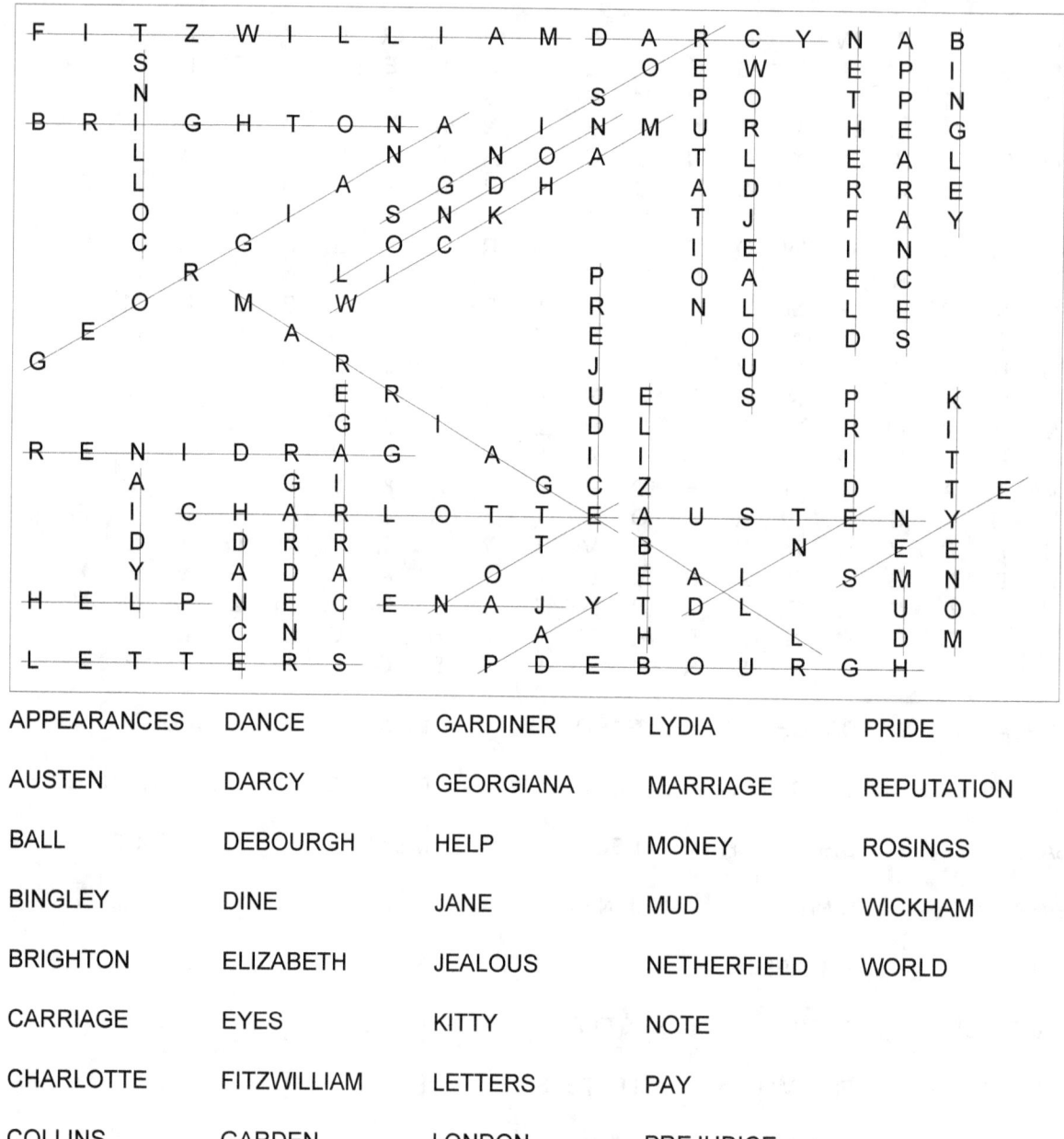

APPEARANCES	DANCE	GARDINER	LYDIA	PRIDE
AUSTEN	DARCY	GEORGIANA	MARRIAGE	REPUTATION
BALL	DEBOURGH	HELP	MONEY	ROSINGS
BINGLEY	DINE	JANE	MUD	WICKHAM
BRIGHTON	ELIZABETH	JEALOUS	NETHERFIELD	WORLD
CARRIAGE	EYES	KITTY	NOTE	
CHARLOTTE	FITZWILLIAM	LETTERS	PAY	
COLLINS	GARDEN	LONDON	PREJUDICE	

Pride & Prejudice Crossword 1

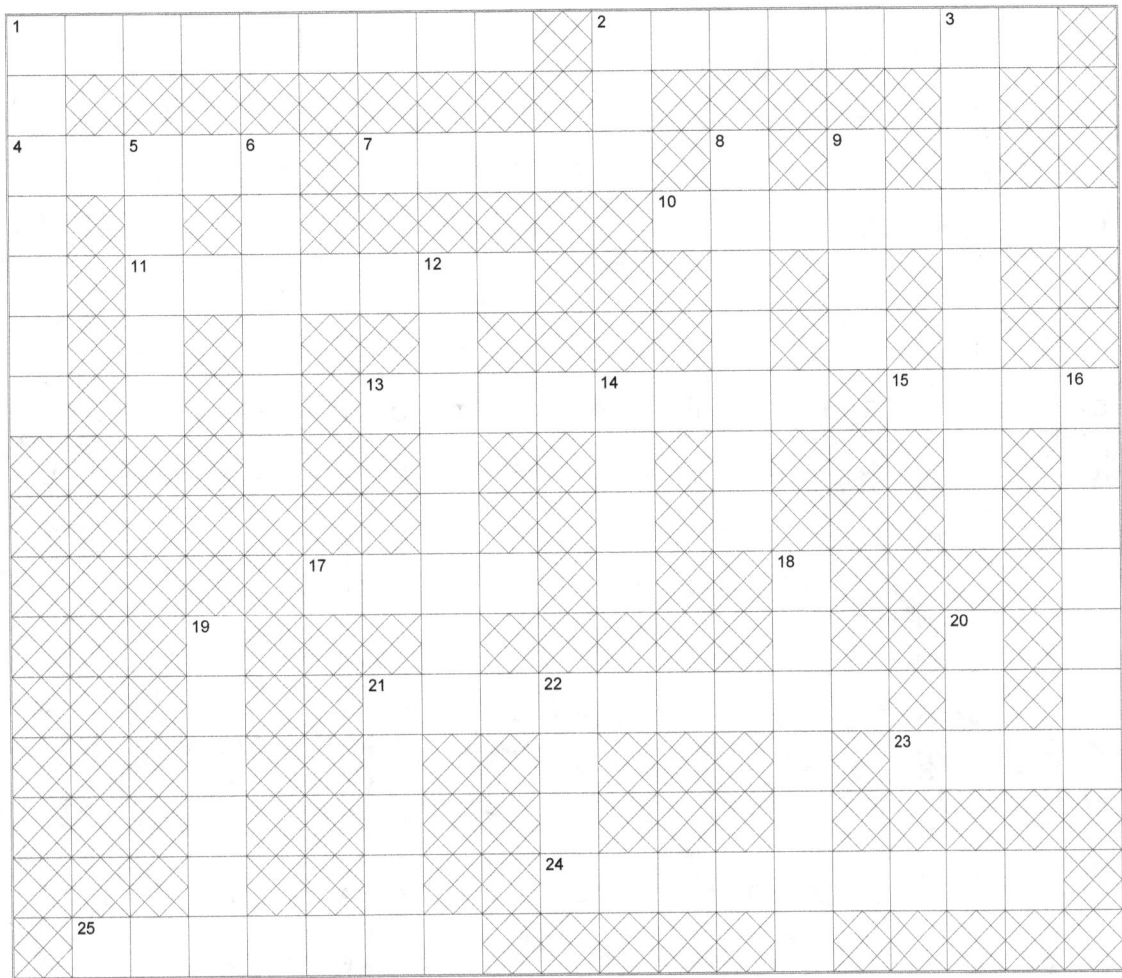

Across
1. She agrees to marry Mr. Collins although she doesn't love him.
2. Mr. Collins disregards Elizabeth's rejection of his ___ proposal.
4. Elopes with Wickham
7. The more I see of the __ the more I am dissatisfied with it.
10. Lady Catherine ___
11. Lady Catherine's home
13. Lydia is invited by Col. Forster's wife to go there.
15. A kind of event where there is dancing
17. Eat dinner
21. Pride and ___
23. Elizabeth's attracted Darcy
24. Frank and independent Bennet daughter
25. Rich man of Netherfield

Down
1. Will inherit Longbourn
2. Elizabeth arrived at Netherfield covered in it.
3. Darcy's sister
5. Owner of Pemberley
6. Author
8. Miss Bingley is ___ that Elizabeth has Darcy's interest.
9. Short letter
12. She warns Elizabeth not to fall in love with Wickham.
14. Darcy ___ed the Bennets; aided
16. Means of communication
18. Military man; gambler
19. A beautiful place to stroll and take walks
20. Darcy had to ___ Wickham's debts.
21. ___ and Prejudice
22. Eldest Bennet daughter

Pride & Prejudice Crossword 1 Answer Key

	1 C	H	A	R	L	O	T	T	E		2 M	A	R	R	I	A	3 G	E	
	O										U						E		
	4 L	5 Y	6 D	I	7 A	W	O	R	L	D	8 J	9 N	O						
	L		A		U					10 D	E	B	O	U	R	G	H		
	I	11 R	O	S	I	12 N	G	S		A		T				G			
	N	C	T			A				L		E				I			
	S	Y	E		13 B	R	14 I	G	H	T	O	N		15 B	A	L	16 L		
					N		D			E		U				N	E		
							I			L		S				A	T		
				17 D	I	N	E			P		18 W					T		
			19 G			E						I			20 P		E		
			A		21 P	R	E	22 J	U	D	I	C	E		A		R		
			R		R			A				K		23 E	Y	E	S		
			D		I			N				H							
			E		D			24 E	L	I	Z	A	B	E	T	H			
		25 B	I	N	G	L	E	Y				M							

Across
1. She agrees to marry Mr. Collins although she doesn't love him.
2. Mr. Collins disregards Elizabeth's rejection of his ___ proposal.
4. Elopes with Wickham
7. The more I see of the __ the more I am dissatisfied with it.
10. Lady Catherine ___
11. Lady Catherine's home
13. Lydia is invited by Col. Forster's wife to go there.
15. A kind of event where there is dancing
17. Eat dinner
21. Pride and ___
23. Elizabeth's attracted Darcy
24. Frank and independent Bennet daughter
25. Rich man of Netherfield

Down
1. Will inherit Longbourn
2. Elizabeth arrived at Netherfield covered in it.
3. Darcy's sister
5. Owner of Pemberley
6. Author
8. Miss Bingley is ___ that Elizabeth has Darcy's interest.
9. Short letter
12. She warns Elizabeth not to fall in love with Wickham.
14. Darcy ___ed the Bennets; aided
16. Means of communication
18. Military man; gambler
19. A beautiful place to stroll and take walks
20. Darcy had to ___ Wickham's debts.
21. ___ and Prejudice
22. Eldest Bennet daughter

Pride & Prejudice Crossword 2

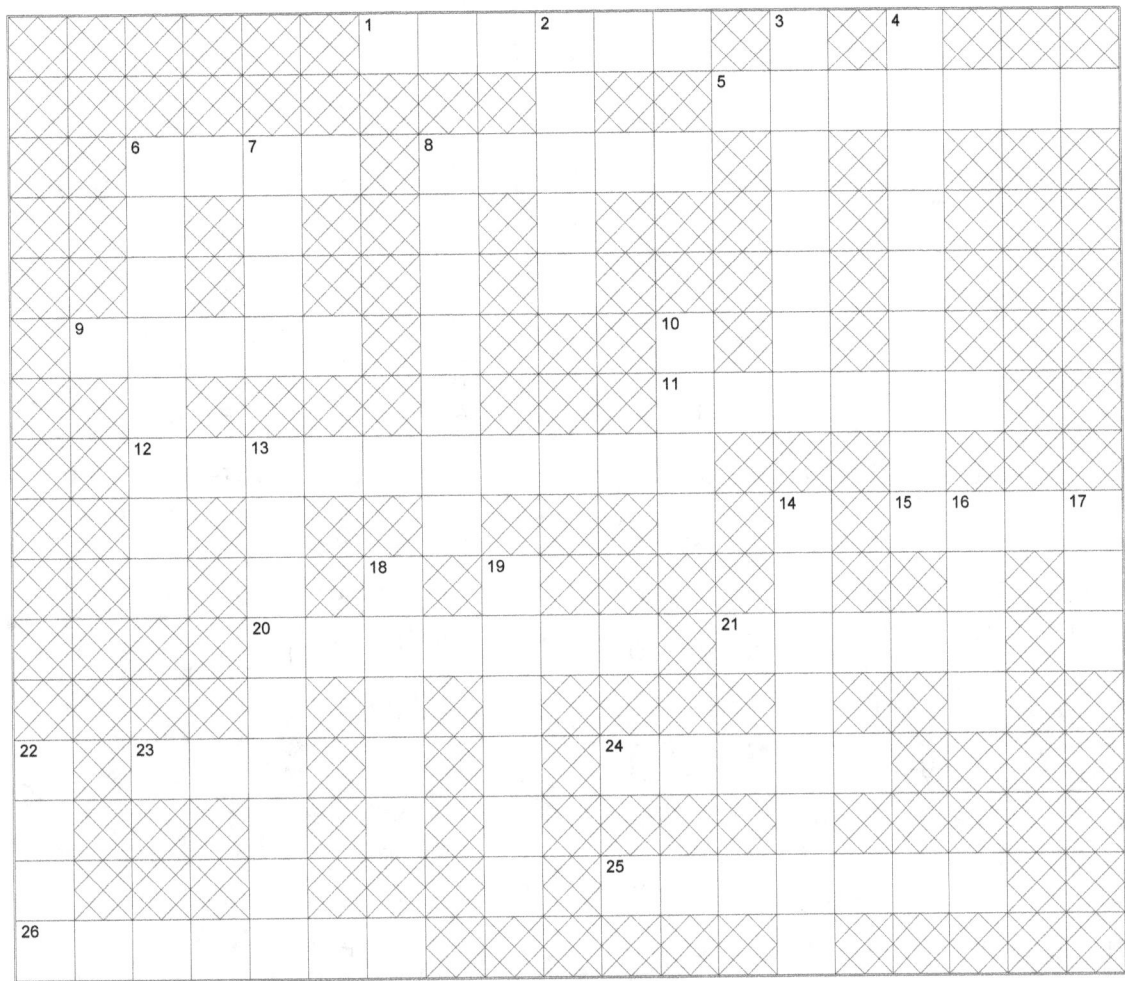

Across
1. A beautiful place to stroll and take walks
5. Will inherit Longbourn
6. Eat dinner
8. The more I see of the ___ the more I am dissatisfied with it.
9. Darcy had lots of it; he was rich.
11. Author
12. The Bennets were concerned about Lydia's ___.
15. Darcy ___ed the Bennets; aided
20. Miss Bingley is ___ that Elizabeth has Darcy's interest.
21. ___ and Prejudice
23. Elizabeth arrived at Netherfield covered in it.
24. Elopes with Wickham
25. Rich man of Netherfield
26. Means of communication

Down
2. Owner of Pemberley
3. Lady Catherine's home
4. Frank and independent Bennet daughter
6. Lady Catherine ___
7. Short letter
8. Military man; gambler
10. Eldest Bennet daughter
13. Pride and ___
14. Means of transportation
16. Elizabeth's attracted Darcy
17. Darcy had to ___ Wickham's debts.
18. One does this at a ball.
19. Town where Lydia and Wickham went
22. A kind of event where there is dancing

Pride & Prejudice Crossword 2 Answer Key

Across
1. A beautiful place to stroll and take walks
5. Will inherit Longbourn
6. Eat dinner
8. The more I see of the ___ the more I am dissatisfied with it.
9. Darcy had lots of it; he was rich.
11. Author
12. The Bennets were concerned about Lydia's ___.
15. Darcy ___ed the Bennets; aided
20. Miss Bingley is ___ that Elizabeth has Darcy's interest.
21. ___ and Prejudice
23. Elizabeth arrived at Netherfield covered in it.
24. Elopes with Wickham
25. Rich man of Netherfield
26. Means of communication

Down
2. Owner of Pemberley
3. Lady Catherine's home
4. Frank and independent Bennet daughter
6. Lady Catherine ___
7. Short letter
8. Military man; gambler
10. Eldest Bennet daughter
13. Pride and ___
14. Means of transportation
16. Elizabeth's attracted Darcy
17. Darcy had to ___ Wickham's debts.
18. One does this at a ball.
19. Town where Lydia and Wickham went
22. A kind of event where there is dancing

Solution Grid

Across: 1. GARDEN, 5. COLLINS, 6. DINE, 8. WORLD, 9. MONEY, 11. AUSTEN, 12. REPUTATION, 15. HELP, 20. JEALOUS, 21. PRIDE, 23. MUD, 24. LYDIA, 25. BINGLEY, 26. LETTERS

Down: 2. DARCY, 3. ROSINGS, 4. ELIZABETH, 6. DEBOURGH, 7. NOTE, 8. WICKHAM, 10. JANE, 13. PREJUDICE, 14. CARRIAGE, 16. EYES, 17. PAY, 18. DANCE, 19. LONDON, 22. BALL

Pride & Prejudice Crossword 3

Across

1. Owner of Pemberley
2. The more I see of the ___ the more I am dissatisfied with it.
5. Darcy had to ___ Wickham's debts.
6. Darcy had lots of it; he was rich.
8. Darcy ___ed the Bennets; aided
9. Lady Catherine ___
13. Darcy's sister
14. Elizabeth arrived at Netherfield covered in it.
16. Elizabeth's attracted Darcy
17. Author
20. Lydia is invited by Col. Forster's wife to go there.
21. Miss Bingley is ___ that Elizabeth has Darcy's interest.
22. Town where Lydia and Wickham went
23. Means of communication

Down

1. One does this at a ball.
2. Military man; gambler
3. Lady Catherine's home
4. A kind of event where there is dancing
7. She agrees to marry Mr. Collins although she doesn't love him.
9. Eat dinner
10. Rich man of Netherfield
11. The Bennets were concerned about Lydia's ___.
12. A beautiful place to stroll and take walks
15. Younger sister under Lydia's influence
18. Short letter
19. ___ and Prejudice
21. Eldest Bennet daughter

Pride & Prejudice Crossword 3 Answer Key

Across
1. Owner of Pemberley
2. The more I see of the __ the more I am dissatisfied with it.
5. Darcy had to ___ Wickham's debts.
6. Darcy had lots of it; he was rich.
8. Darcy ___ed the Bennets; aided
9. Lady Catherine ___
13. Darcy's sister
14. Elizabeth arrived at Netherfield covered in it.
16. Elizabeth's attracted Darcy
17. Author
20. Lydia is invited by Col. Forster's wife to go there.
21. Miss Bingley is ___ that Elizabeth has Darcy's interest.
22. Town where Lydia and Wickham went
23. Means of communication

Down
1. One does this at a ball.
2. Military man; gambler
3. Lady Catherine's home
4. A kind of event where there is dancing
7. She agrees to marry Mr. Collins although she doesn't love him.
9. Eat dinner
10. Rich man of Netherfield
11. The Bennets were concerned about Lydia's ___.
12. A beautiful place to stroll and take walks
15. Younger sister under Lydia's influence
18. Short letter
19. ___ and Prejudice
21. Eldest Bennet daughter

Pride & Prejudice Crossword 4

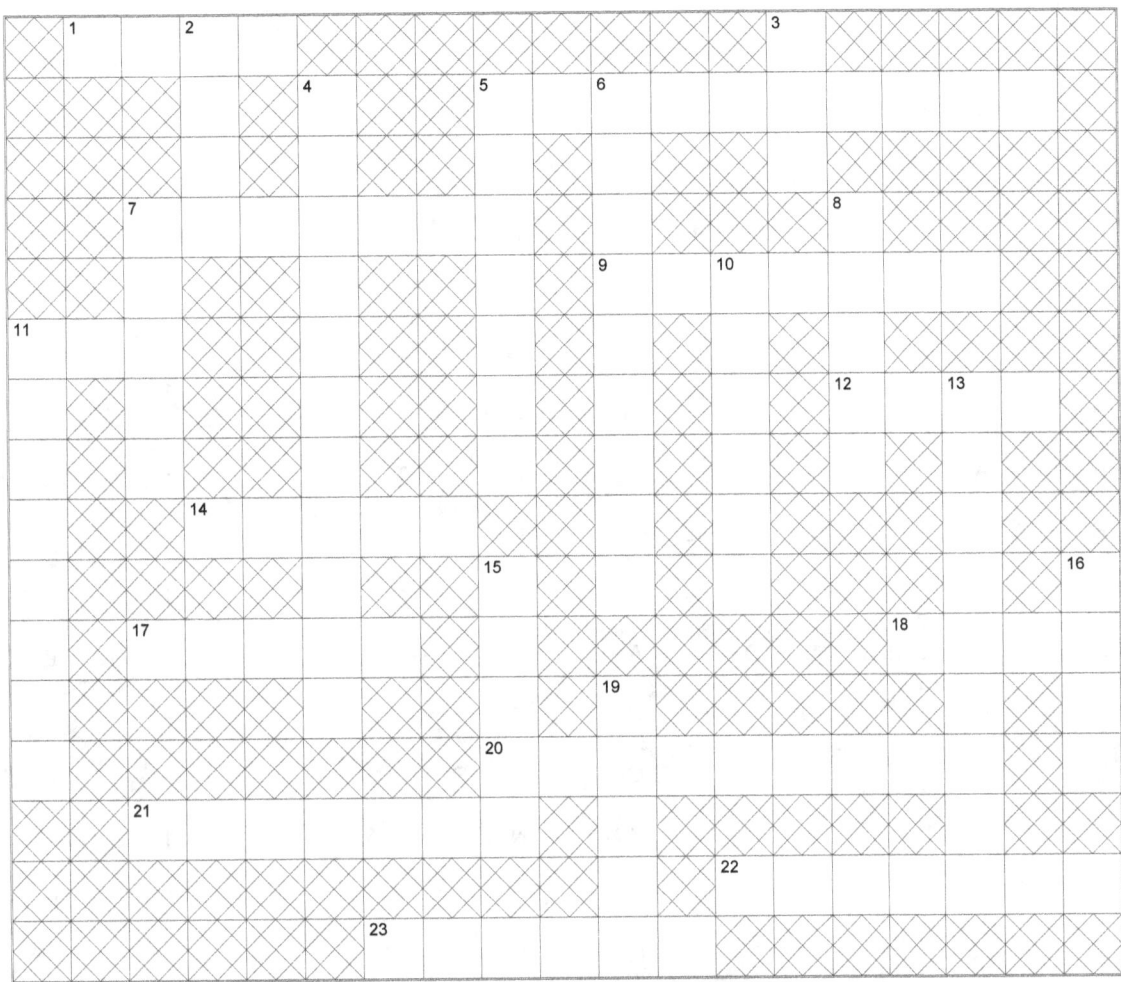

Across
1. Eat dinner
5. The Bennets were concerned about Lydia's ___.
7. Means of communication
9. Miss Bingley is ___ that Elizabeth has Darcy's interest.
11. Elizabeth arrived at Netherfield covered in it.
12. Elizabeth's attracted Darcy
14. ___ and Prejudice
17. The more I see of the ___ the more I am dissatisfied with it.
18. Eldest Bennet daughter
20. She agrees to marry Mr. Collins although she doesn't love him.
21. Rich man of Netherfield
22. Military man; gambler
23. A beautiful place to stroll and take walks

Down
2. Short letter
3. Darcy had to ___ Wickham's debts.
4. Mrs. Bennet wants Eliz. & Jane to stay overnight at ___ Hall.
5. Lady Catherine's home
6. Pride and ___
7. Elopes with Wickham
8. Darcy had lots of it; he was rich.
10. Author
11. Mr. Collins disregards Elizabeth's rejection of his ___ proposal.
13. Frank and independent Bennet daughter
15. Owner of Pemberley
16. Darcy ___ed the Bennets; aided
19. One does this at a ball.

Pride & Prejudice Crossword 4 Answer Key

Across
1. Eat dinner
5. The Bennets were concerned about Lydia's ___.
7. Means of communication
9. Miss Bingley is ___ that Elizabeth has Darcy's interest.
11. Elizabeth arrived at Netherfield covered in it.
12. Elizabeth's attracted Darcy
14. ___ and Prejudice
17. The more I see of the ___ the more I am dissatisfied with it.
18. Eldest Bennet daughter
20. She agrees to marry Mr. Collins although she doesn't love him.
21. Rich man of Netherfield
22. Military man; gambler
23. A beautiful place to stroll and take walks

Down
2. Short letter
3. Darcy had to ___ Wickham's debts.
4. Mrs. Bennet wants Eliz. & Jane to stay overnight at ___ Hall.
5. Lady Catherine's home
6. Pride and ___
7. Elopes with Wickham
8. Darcy had lots of it; he was rich.
10. Author
11. Mr. Collins disregards Elizabeth's rejection of his ___ proposal.
13. Frank and independent Bennet daughter
15. Owner of Pemberley
16. Darcy ___ed the Bennets; aided
19. One does this at a ball.

Grid Answers:

Across: 1. DINE, 5. REPUTATION, 7. LETTERS, 9. JEALOUS, 11. MUD, 12. EYES, 14. PRIDE, 17. WORLD, 18. JANE, 20. CHARLOTTE, 21. BINGLEY, 22. WICKHAM, 23. GARDEN

Down: 2. NOTE, 3. PAY, 4. NETHERFIELD, 5. ROSINGS, 6. PREJUDICE, 7. LYDIA, 8. MONEY, 10. AUSTEN, 11. MARRIAGE, 13. ELIZABETH, 15. DARCY, 16. HELPED, 19. DANCE

Pride & Prejudice

MUD	WORLD	HELP	KITTY	BRIGHTON
CARRIAGE	JEALOUS	DANCE	WICKHAM	NETHERFIELD
DINE	LETTERS	FREE SPACE	COLLINS	LYDIA
APPEARANCES	MARRIAGE	NOTE	BINGLEY	DARCY
GARDINER	PAY	DEBOURGH	FITZWILLIAM	PRIDE

Pride & Prejudice

GARDEN	BALL	ELIZABETH	AUSTEN	CHARLOTTE
EYES	MONEY	LONDON	JANE	ROSINGS
REPUTATION	GEORGIANA	FREE SPACE	FITZWILLIAM	DEBOURGH
PAY	GARDINER	DARCY	BINGLEY	NOTE
MARRIAGE	APPEARANCES	LYDIA	COLLINS	PREJUDICE

Pride & Prejudice

LONDON	EYES	DARCY	LYDIA	JANE
DEBOURGH	CARRIAGE	FITZWILLIAM	HELP	WORLD
JEALOUS	GARDEN	FREE SPACE	PRIDE	BRIGHTON
KITTY	NETHERFIELD	DINE	GEORGIANA	COLLINS
AUSTEN	PAY	LETTERS	REPUTATION	ELIZABETH

Pride & Prejudice

NOTE	MUD	CHARLOTTE	GARDINER	APPEARANCES
PREJUDICE	DANCE	WICKHAM	BINGLEY	MONEY
ROSINGS	BALL	FREE SPACE	REPUTATION	LETTERS
PAY	AUSTEN	COLLINS	GEORGIANA	DINE
NETHERFIELD	KITTY	BRIGHTON	PRIDE	MARRIAGE

Pride & Prejudice

LETTERS	BALL	GARDEN	JANE	NETHERFIELD
CARRIAGE	COLLINS	WICKHAM	KITTY	BINGLEY
MARRIAGE	MUD	FREE SPACE	MONEY	LONDON
DARCY	PREJUDICE	GARDINER	WORLD	HELP
DEBOURGH	EYES	AUSTEN	ROSINGS	ELIZABETH

Pride & Prejudice

PAY	APPEARANCES	LYDIA	DANCE	DINE
CHARLOTTE	JEALOUS	FITZWILLIAM	PRIDE	NOTE
REPUTATION	BRIGHTON	FREE SPACE	ROSINGS	AUSTEN
EYES	DEBOURGH	HELP	WORLD	GARDINER
PREJUDICE	DARCY	LONDON	MONEY	GEORGIANA

Pride & Prejudice

ROSINGS	PRIDE	WORLD	DANCE	FITZWILLIAM
AUSTEN	NETHERFIELD	MUD	DEBOURGH	MONEY
PREJUDICE	REPUTATION	FREE SPACE	HELP	BINGLEY
LYDIA	DARCY	NOTE	GARDEN	WICKHAM
ELIZABETH	KITTY	COLLINS	JEALOUS	MARRIAGE

Pride & Prejudice

BALL	DINE	EYES	JANE	BRIGHTON
LONDON	PAY	LETTERS	APPEARANCES	CARRIAGE
CHARLOTTE	GARDINER	FREE SPACE	JEALOUS	COLLINS
KITTY	ELIZABETH	WICKHAM	GARDEN	NOTE
DARCY	LYDIA	BINGLEY	HELP	GEORGIANA

Pride & Prejudice

ELIZABETH	BALL	CARRIAGE	EYES	APPEARANCES
JEALOUS	LETTERS	DANCE	AUSTEN	HELP
REPUTATION	KITTY	FREE SPACE	MONEY	GARDINER
PREJUDICE	DINE	COLLINS	GARDEN	DARCY
ROSINGS	PAY	BINGLEY	LYDIA	WORLD

Pride & Prejudice

NETHERFIELD	JANE	LONDON	CHARLOTTE	NOTE
PRIDE	WICKHAM	GEORGIANA	FITZWILLIAM	MUD
DEBOURGH	MARRIAGE	FREE SPACE	LYDIA	BINGLEY
PAY	ROSINGS	DARCY	GARDEN	COLLINS
DINE	PREJUDICE	GARDINER	MONEY	BRIGHTON

Pride & Prejudice

MUD	DEBOURGH	HELP	ELIZABETH	MARRIAGE
EYES	GARDINER	CARRIAGE	PAY	MONEY
LYDIA	LONDON	FREE SPACE	JANE	AUSTEN
BRIGHTON	PRIDE	WORLD	CHARLOTTE	WICKHAM
APPEARANCES	FITZWILLIAM	GEORGIANA	NETHERFIELD	DANCE

Pride & Prejudice

DINE	BALL	KITTY	GARDEN	DARCY
NOTE	COLLINS	BINGLEY	REPUTATION	ROSINGS
JEALOUS	PREJUDICE	FREE SPACE	NETHERFIELD	GEORGIANA
FITZWILLIAM	APPEARANCES	WICKHAM	CHARLOTTE	WORLD
PRIDE	BRIGHTON	AUSTEN	JANE	LETTERS

Pride & Prejudice

WICKHAM	HELP	MARRIAGE	REPUTATION	GARDEN
AUSTEN	NOTE	DINE	WORLD	DEBOURGH
DANCE	BRIGHTON	FREE SPACE	JEALOUS	NETHERFIELD
GEORGIANA	BINGLEY	GARDINER	ELIZABETH	LETTERS
ROSINGS	PREJUDICE	EYES	APPEARANCES	LYDIA

Pride & Prejudice

JANE	MUD	KITTY	BALL	CARRIAGE
MONEY	LONDON	FITZWILLIAM	PAY	DARCY
CHARLOTTE	PRIDE	FREE SPACE	APPEARANCES	EYES
PREJUDICE	ROSINGS	LETTERS	ELIZABETH	GARDINER
BINGLEY	GEORGIANA	NETHERFIELD	JEALOUS	COLLINS

Pride & Prejudice

AUSTEN	DEBOURGH	BALL	KITTY	COLLINS
REPUTATION	GARDEN	MONEY	FITZWILLIAM	ELIZABETH
GEORGIANA	JANE	FREE SPACE	HELP	WORLD
EYES	CARRIAGE	MUD	GARDINER	LETTERS
APPEARANCES	JEALOUS	LONDON	BINGLEY	DINE

Pride & Prejudice

ROSINGS	BRIGHTON	PAY	LYDIA	NOTE
WICKHAM	DARCY	DANCE	NETHERFIELD	CHARLOTTE
PRIDE	MARRIAGE	FREE SPACE	BINGLEY	LONDON
JEALOUS	APPEARANCES	LETTERS	GARDINER	MUD
CARRIAGE	EYES	WORLD	HELP	PREJUDICE

Pride & Prejudice

FITZWILLIAM	MARRIAGE	PREJUDICE	GEORGIANA	LETTERS
REPUTATION	DARCY	AUSTEN	EYES	MONEY
CHARLOTTE	KITTY	FREE SPACE	ROSINGS	LYDIA
NETHERFIELD	BINGLEY	GARDINER	JANE	MUD
DANCE	HELP	COLLINS	CARRIAGE	BRIGHTON

Pride & Prejudice

DINE	WORLD	WICKHAM	ELIZABETH	DEBOURGH
APPEARANCES	LONDON	JEALOUS	PRIDE	BALL
NOTE	GARDEN	FREE SPACE	CARRIAGE	COLLINS
HELP	DANCE	MUD	JANE	GARDINER
BINGLEY	NETHERFIELD	LYDIA	ROSINGS	PAY

Pride & Prejudice

ELIZABETH	NOTE	CARRIAGE	PAY	ROSINGS
MUD	DEBOURGH	GARDINER	COLLINS	HELP
WORLD	REPUTATION	FREE SPACE	NETHERFIELD	WICKHAM
LYDIA	BALL	LONDON	BINGLEY	DARCY
FITZWILLIAM	LETTERS	DANCE	GEORGIANA	CHARLOTTE

Pride & Prejudice

MARRIAGE	GARDEN	JANE	KITTY	DINE
APPEARANCES	JEALOUS	BRIGHTON	AUSTEN	MONEY
EYES	PREJUDICE	FREE SPACE	GEORGIANA	DANCE
LETTERS	FITZWILLIAM	DARCY	BINGLEY	LONDON
BALL	LYDIA	WICKHAM	NETHERFIELD	PRIDE

Pride & Prejudice

GARDINER	LETTERS	CHARLOTTE	APPEARANCES	REPUTATION
BRIGHTON	ROSINGS	NETHERFIELD	NOTE	LYDIA
HELP	DANCE	FREE SPACE	EYES	MARRIAGE
PREJUDICE	DEBOURGH	JANE	JEALOUS	MUD
KITTY	ELIZABETH	COLLINS	AUSTEN	WORLD

Pride & Prejudice

BINGLEY	DINE	PRIDE	FITZWILLIAM	GEORGIANA
PAY	GARDEN	BALL	DARCY	WICKHAM
LONDON	CARRIAGE	FREE SPACE	AUSTEN	COLLINS
ELIZABETH	KITTY	MUD	JEALOUS	JANE
DEBOURGH	PREJUDICE	MARRIAGE	EYES	MONEY

Pride & Prejudice

ELIZABETH	AUSTEN	ROSINGS	PRIDE	APPEARANCES
NOTE	PAY	DANCE	CHARLOTTE	BALL
HELP	KITTY	FREE SPACE	BINGLEY	LETTERS
MUD	WORLD	GEORGIANA	DARCY	MONEY
LONDON	WICKHAM	JANE	MARRIAGE	NETHERFIELD

Pride & Prejudice

REPUTATION	GARDINER	DEBOURGH	DINE	EYES
CARRIAGE	JEALOUS	BRIGHTON	COLLINS	LYDIA
FITZWILLIAM	GARDEN	FREE SPACE	MARRIAGE	JANE
WICKHAM	LONDON	MONEY	DARCY	GEORGIANA
WORLD	MUD	LETTERS	BINGLEY	PREJUDICE

Pride & Prejudice

JANE	APPEARANCES	DARCY	NETHERFIELD	HELP
PRIDE	LONDON	ROSINGS	GARDEN	WICKHAM
MARRIAGE	GEORGIANA	FREE SPACE	LYDIA	LETTERS
EYES	COLLINS	BALL	MUD	JEALOUS
PAY	REPUTATION	MONEY	DANCE	NOTE

Pride & Prejudice

BRIGHTON	GARDINER	FITZWILLIAM	AUSTEN	BINGLEY
KITTY	CHARLOTTE	DEBOURGH	PREJUDICE	WORLD
DINE	ELIZABETH	FREE SPACE	DANCE	MONEY
REPUTATION	PAY	JEALOUS	MUD	BALL
COLLINS	EYES	LETTERS	LYDIA	CARRIAGE

Pride & Prejudice

BINGLEY	CHARLOTTE	MUD	DEBOURGH	PAY
PRIDE	NOTE	ELIZABETH	DINE	JANE
PREJUDICE	LYDIA	FREE SPACE	JEALOUS	BALL
WORLD	COLLINS	REPUTATION	AUSTEN	ROSINGS
KITTY	CARRIAGE	FITZWILLIAM	LONDON	GEORGIANA

Pride & Prejudice

EYES	APPEARANCES	DANCE	HELP	LETTERS
NETHERFIELD	BRIGHTON	GARDINER	DARCY	MONEY
GARDEN	MARRIAGE	FREE SPACE	LONDON	FITZWILLIAM
CARRIAGE	KITTY	ROSINGS	AUSTEN	REPUTATION
COLLINS	WORLD	BALL	JEALOUS	WICKHAM

Pride & Prejudice

WICKHAM	REPUTATION	LONDON	DINE	LETTERS
HELP	DANCE	DARCY	GARDEN	MARRIAGE
GARDINER	MONEY	FREE SPACE	PAY	EYES
DEBOURGH	BALL	GEORGIANA	PRIDE	LYDIA
ROSINGS	JANE	COLLINS	AUSTEN	KITTY

Pride & Prejudice

APPEARANCES	WORLD	MUD	BINGLEY	PREJUDICE
NOTE	NETHERFIELD	FITZWILLIAM	JEALOUS	CARRIAGE
CHARLOTTE	BRIGHTON	FREE SPACE	AUSTEN	COLLINS
JANE	ROSINGS	LYDIA	PRIDE	GEORGIANA
BALL	DEBOURGH	EYES	PAY	ELIZABETH

Pride & Prejudice

PAY	CHARLOTTE	GARDEN	JEALOUS	EYES
REPUTATION	BINGLEY	LETTERS	HELP	LYDIA
WICKHAM	APPEARANCES	FREE SPACE	KITTY	WORLD
GARDINER	PRIDE	ROSINGS	GEORGIANA	MUD
BRIGHTON	DEBOURGH	MONEY	AUSTEN	DARCY

Pride & Prejudice

CARRIAGE	PREJUDICE	NETHERFIELD	BALL	MARRIAGE
DANCE	NOTE	COLLINS	LONDON	JANE
FITZWILLIAM	DINE	FREE SPACE	AUSTEN	MONEY
DEBOURGH	BRIGHTON	MUD	GEORGIANA	ROSINGS
PRIDE	GARDINER	WORLD	KITTY	ELIZABETH

Pride & Prejudice Vocabulary Word List

No.	Word	Clue/Definition
1.	AFFABILITY	Quality of being pleasant & easy to speak with
2.	AFFINITY	Natural attraction to
3.	ALACRITY	Cheerful willingness
4.	APPROBATION	Approval
5.	ASCERTAINING	Finding out; discovering
6.	ASPIRE	Desire; have an ambition or goal
7.	AUGMENTED	Added
8.	BREVITY	Shortness; quality of being short in duration
9.	CAPRICE	Impulsive change of mind
10.	CIRCUMSPECTION	Prudence
11.	COGENT	Convincing
12.	CONJECTURE	Guess
13.	CONJUGAL	Relating to marriage
14.	COPSE	Thicket of small trees
15.	DEFER	Postpone
16.	DERISION	Ridicule
17.	DESTITUTE	Lacking; poor
18.	DILATORY	Tending to delay
19.	DIMINUTION	Reduction
20.	ECSTASY	Intense joy
21.	EFFICACY	Effectiveness
22.	EFFUSION	Unrestrained outpouring of speech
23.	ENGROSSED	Totally occupied
24.	ENTREATIES	Pleas
25.	ENVY	Desire for the possessions of others
26.	FASTIDIOUS	Meticulous; concerned with details; difficult to please
27.	IMPERTINENT	Improperly bold or forward
28.	IMPLACABLE	Impossible to appease or please
29.	IMPRUDENCE	Characteristic of making unwise decisions
30.	IMPUTE	Credit
31.	INCUMBENT	Imposed as a duty or obligation
32.	INJUNCTIONS	Commands; orders
33.	INSOLENT	Insulting; disrespectful; rude
34.	INVECTIVES	Abusive language
35.	MERCENARY	Motivated by money or material goods
36.	OBEISANCE	Gesture of deference or homage
37.	OBLIGE	Do a favor or service for
38.	OMEN	A sign of the future
39.	OSTENTATIOUS	Pretentious; pompous
40.	PANEGYRIC	Praise; compliment
41.	PECUNIARY	Relating to money
42.	PERPETUALLY	Continually; constantly
43.	PLIANCY	Flexibility
44.	PROFLIGATE	Wasteful; extravagant
45.	PROPITIOUS	Favorable
46.	PURSUED	Advanced; chased after
47.	QUERULOUS	Grumbling; complaining
48.	RECTITUDE	Moral uprightness
49.	REPINE	To be discontented or in low spirits
50.	REQUITED	Repaid
51.	SAGACITY	Judgement; wisdom

Pride & Prejudice Vocabulary Word List Continued

No.	Word	Clue/Definition
52.	SANGUINE	Cheerfully confident; optimistic
53.	SCRUPLE	Hesitate as a result of conscience
54.	SUPERCILIOUS	Haughty; disdainful
55.	TACIT	Implied by action
56.	TACITURN	Not talkative
57.	TITHES	Money given to support the clergy
58.	TRACTABLE	Manageable; easily handled
59.	TRIFLING	Of little significance
60.	VAGUE	Unclear; not well defined
61.	VALID	Legal and binding
62.	VERACITY	Truthfulness
63.	VOGUE	Fashion; popularity
64.	VOID	Empty
65.	VOLUBILITY	Fluency of speech

Pride & Prejudice Vocabulary Fill In The Blanks 1

_____ 1. Grumbling; complaining

_____ 2. Repaid

_____ 3. Legal and binding

_____ 4. Improperly bold or forward

_____ 5. Fluency of speech

_____ 6. Implied by action

_____ 7. Judgement; wisdom

_____ 8. Meticulous; concerned with details; difficult to please

_____ 9. Continually; constantly

_____ 10. Insulting; disrespectful; rude

_____ 11. Pretentious; pompous

_____ 12. Relating to money

_____ 13. Impulsive change of mind

_____ 14. Motivated by money or material goods

_____ 15. Not talkative

_____ 16. Desire; have an ambition or goal

_____ 17. Tending to delay

_____ 18. Cheerful willingness

_____ 19. Quality of being pleasant & easy to speak with

_____ 20. A sign of the future

Pride & Prejudice Vocabulary Fill In The Blanks 1 Answer Key

QUERULOUS	1. Grumbling; complaining
REQUITED	2. Repaid
VALID	3. Legal and binding
IMPERTINENT	4. Improperly bold or forward
VOLUBILITY	5. Fluency of speech
TACIT	6. Implied by action
SAGACITY	7. Judgement; wisdom
FASTIDIOUS	8. Meticulous; concerned with details; difficult to please
PERPETUALLY	9. Continually; constantly
INSOLENT	10. Insulting; disrespectful; rude
OSTENTATIOUS	11. Pretentious; pompous
PECUNIARY	12. Relating to money
CAPRICE	13. Impulsive change of mind
MERCENARY	14. Motivated by money or material goods
TACITURN	15. Not talkative
ASPIRE	16. Desire; have an ambition or goal
DILATORY	17. Tending to delay
ALACRITY	18. Cheerful willingness
AFFABILITY	19. Quality of being pleasant & easy to speak with
OMEN	20. A sign of the future

Pride & Prejudice Vocabulary Fill In The Blanks 2

_____ 1. Not talkative

_____ 2. Convincing

_____ 3. Intense joy

_____ 4. Reduction

_____ 5. Pretentious; pompous

_____ 6. Postpone

_____ 7. Credit

_____ 8. Of little significance

_____ 9. To be discontented or in low spirits

_____ 10. Continually; constantly

_____ 11. Praise; compliment

_____ 12. Shortness; quality of being short in duration

_____ 13. Pleas

_____ 14. Totally occupied

_____ 15. Desire for the possessions of others

_____ 16. Advanced; chased after

_____ 17. Imposed as a duty or obligation

_____ 18. Lacking; poor

_____ 19. Judgement; wisdom

_____ 20. Repaid

Pride & Prejudice Vocabulary Fill In The Blanks 2 Answer Key

TACITURN	1. Not talkative
COGENT	2. Convincing
ECSTASY	3. Intense joy
DIMINUTION	4. Reduction
OSTENTATIOUS	5. Pretentious; pompous
DEFER	6. Postpone
IMPUTE	7. Credit
TRIFLING	8. Of little significance
REPINE	9. To be discontented or in low spirits
PERPETUALLY	10. Continually; constantly
PANEGYRIC	11. Praise; compliment
BREVITY	12. Shortness; quality of being short in duration
ENTREATIES	13. Pleas
ENGROSSED	14. Totally occupied
ENVY	15. Desire for the possessions of others
PURSUED	16. Advanced; chased after
INCUMBENT	17. Imposed as a duty or obligation
DESTITUTE	18. Lacking; poor
SAGACITY	19. Judgement; wisdom
REQUITED	20. Repaid

Pride & Prejudice Vocabulary Fill In The Blanks 3

1. Cheerfully confident; optimistic
2. Tending to delay
3. Wasteful; extravagant
4. Finding out; discovering
5. Advanced; chased after
6. Grumbling; complaining
7. Desire; have an ambition or goal
8. Impulsive change of mind
9. Impossible to appease or please
10. Effectiveness
11. Legal and binding
12. Fashion; popularity
13. Empty
14. Repaid
15. Pretentious; pompous
16. Haughty; disdainful
17. Motivated by money or material goods
18. Manageable; easily handled
19. Unrestrained outpouring of speech
20. Prudence

Pride & Prejudice Vocabulary Fill In The Blanks 3 Answer Key

SANGUINE	1. Cheerfully confident; optimistic
DILATORY	2. Tending to delay
PROFLIGATE	3. Wasteful; extravagant
ASCERTAINING	4. Finding out; discovering
PURSUED	5. Advanced; chased after
QUERULOUS	6. Grumbling; complaining
ASPIRE	7. Desire; have an ambition or goal
CAPRICE	8. Impulsive change of mind
IMPLACABLE	9. Impossible to appease or please
EFFICACY	10. Effectiveness
VALID	11. Legal and binding
VOGUE	12. Fashion; popularity
VOID	13. Empty
REQUITED	14. Repaid
OSTENTATIOUS	15. Pretentious; pompous
SUPERCILIOUS	16. Haughty; disdainful
MERCENARY	17. Motivated by money or material goods
TRACTABLE	18. Manageable; easily handled
EFFUSION	19. Unrestrained outpouring of speech
CIRCUMSPECTION	20. Prudence

Pride & Prejudice Vocabulary Fill In The Blanks 4

_____ 1. Desire for the possessions of others

_____ 2. Legal and binding

_____ 3. Imposed as a duty or obligation

_____ 4. Tending to delay

_____ 5. Intense joy

_____ 6. Praise; compliment

_____ 7. Finding out; discovering

_____ 8. Ridicule

_____ 9. Impossible to appease or please

_____ 10. Effectiveness

_____ 11. Commands; orders

_____ 12. Fluency of speech

_____ 13. Flexibility

_____ 14. Money given to support the clergy

_____ 15. Totally occupied

_____ 16. Continually; constantly

_____ 17. Truthfulness

_____ 18. Natural attraction to

_____ 19. Judgement; wisdom

_____ 20. Empty

Pride & Prejudice Vocabulary Fill In The Blanks 4 Answer Key

ENVY	1. Desire for the possessions of others
VALID	2. Legal and binding
INCUMBENT	3. Imposed as a duty or obligation
DILATORY	4. Tending to delay
ECSTASY	5. Intense joy
PANEGYRIC	6. Praise; compliment
ASCERTAINING	7. Finding out; discovering
DERISION	8. Ridicule
IMPLACABLE	9. Impossible to appease or please
EFFICACY	10. Effectiveness
INJUNCTIONS	11. Commands; orders
VOLUBILITY	12. Fluency of speech
PLIANCY	13. Flexibility
TITHES	14. Money given to support the clergy
ENGROSSED	15. Totally occupied
PERPETUALLY	16. Continually; constantly
VERACITY	17. Truthfulness
AFFINITY	18. Natural attraction to
SAGACITY	19. Judgement; wisdom
VOID	20. Empty

Pride & Prejudice Vocabulary Matching 1

___ 1. TACIT
___ 2. AFFINITY
___ 3. AUGMENTED
___ 4. EFFUSION
___ 5. DERISION
___ 6. OSTENTATIOUS
___ 7. INVECTIVES
___ 8. TRIFLING
___ 9. PROPITIOUS
___10. VOGUE
___11. VAGUE
___12. TRACTABLE
___13. COGENT
___14. SCRUPLE
___15. VOLUBILITY
___16. SAGACITY
___17. PERPETUALLY
___18. PLIANCY
___19. RECTITUDE
___20. SANGUINE
___21. TITHES
___22. REQUITED
___23. DESTITUTE
___24. DILATORY
___25. CONJECTURE

A. Fluency of speech
B. Of little significance
C. Lacking; poor
D. Added
E. Continually; constantly
F. Moral uprightness
G. Manageable; easily handled
H. Favorable
I. Abusive language
J. Pretentious; pompous
K. Tending to delay
L. Unrestrained outpouring of speech
M. Flexibility
N. Guess
O. Natural attraction to
P. Repaid
Q. Convincing
R. Hesitate as a result of conscience
S. Unclear; not well defined
T. Fashion; popularity
U. Judgement; wisdom
V. Implied by action
W. Ridicule
X. Cheerfully confident; optimistic
Y. Money given to support the clergy

Pride & Prejudice Vocabulary Matching 1 Answer Key

V - 1. TACIT		A. Fluency of speech
O - 2. AFFINITY		B. Of little significance
D - 3. AUGMENTED		C. Lacking; poor
L - 4. EFFUSION		D. Added
W - 5. DERISION		E. Continually; constantly
J - 6. OSTENTATIOUS		F. Moral uprightness
I - 7. INVECTIVES		G. Manageable; easily handled
B - 8. TRIFLING		H. Favorable
H - 9. PROPITIOUS		I. Abusive language
T - 10. VOGUE		J. Pretentious; pompous
S - 11. VAGUE		K. Tending to delay
G - 12. TRACTABLE		L. Unrestrained outpouring of speech
Q - 13. COGENT		M. Flexibility
R - 14. SCRUPLE		N. Guess
A - 15. VOLUBILITY		O. Natural attraction to
U - 16. SAGACITY		P. Repaid
E - 17. PERPETUALLY		Q. Convincing
M - 18. PLIANCY		R. Hesitate as a result of conscience
F - 19. RECTITUDE		S. Unclear; not well defined
X - 20. SANGUINE		T. Fashion; popularity
Y - 21. TITHES		U. Judgement; wisdom
P - 22. REQUITED		V. Implied by action
C - 23. DESTITUTE		W. Ridicule
K - 24. DILATORY		X. Cheerfully confident; optimistic
N - 25. CONJECTURE		Y. Money given to support the clergy

Pride & Prejudice Vocabulary Matching 2

___ 1. CAPRICE   A. Characteristic of making unwise decisions
___ 2. PROPITIOUS   B. Favorable
___ 3. FASTIDIOUS   C. Thicket of small trees
___ 4. QUERULOUS   D. Lacking; poor
___ 5. IMPLACABLE   E. Quality of being pleasant & easy to speak with
___ 6. DESTITUTE   F. Gesture of deference or homage
___ 7. PURSUED   G. Grumbling; complaining
___ 8. CONJECTURE   H. Judgement; wisdom
___ 9. OBEISANCE   I. Of little significance
___10. IMPUTE   J. Reduction
___11. DIMINUTION   K. Legal and binding
___12. DERISION   L. Unrestrained outpouring of speech
___13. TRIFLING   M. Unclear; not well defined
___14. AFFABILITY   N. A sign of the future
___15. OMEN   O. Guess
___16. SAGACITY   P. Impulsive change of mind
___17. CIRCUMSPECTION Q. Ridicule
___18. EFFUSION   R. Meticulous; concerned with details; difficult to please
___19. VAGUE   S. Added
___20. IMPRUDENCE   T. Impossible to appease or please
___21. OSTENTATIOUS   U. Prudence
___22. VALID   V. Credit
___23. AUGMENTED   W. Commands; orders
___24. INJUNCTIONS   X. Pretentious; pompous
___25. COPSE   Y. Advanced; chased after

Pride & Prejudice Vocabulary Matching 2 Answer Key

P - 1.	CAPRICE	A. Characteristic of making unwise decisions
B - 2.	PROPITIOUS	B. Favorable
R - 3.	FASTIDIOUS	C. Thicket of small trees
G - 4.	QUERULOUS	D. Lacking; poor
T - 5.	IMPLACABLE	E. Quality of being pleasant & easy to speak with
D - 6.	DESTITUTE	F. Gesture of deference or homage
Y - 7.	PURSUED	G. Grumbling; complaining
O - 8.	CONJECTURE	H. Judgement; wisdom
F - 9.	OBEISANCE	I. Of little significance
V - 10.	IMPUTE	J. Reduction
J - 11.	DIMINUTION	K. Legal and binding
Q - 12.	DERISION	L. Unrestrained outpouring of speech
I - 13.	TRIFLING	M. Unclear; not well defined
E - 14.	AFFABILITY	N. A sign of the future
N - 15.	OMEN	O. Guess
H - 16.	SAGACITY	P. Impulsive change of mind
U - 17.	CIRCUMSPECTION	Q. Ridicule
L - 18.	EFFUSION	R. Meticulous; concerned with details; difficult to please
M - 19.	VAGUE	S. Added
A - 20.	IMPRUDENCE	T. Impossible to appease or please
X - 21.	OSTENTATIOUS	U. Prudence
K - 22.	VALID	V. Credit
S - 23.	AUGMENTED	W. Commands; orders
W - 24.	INJUNCTIONS	X. Pretentious; pompous
C - 25.	COPSE	Y. Advanced; chased after

Pride & Prejudice Vocabulary Matching 3

___ 1. INVECTIVES   A. Haughty; disdainful
___ 2. DEFER   B. Implied by action
___ 3. VOID   C. Legal and binding
___ 4. IMPUTE   D. Moral uprightness
___ 5. TITHES   E. Impossible to appease or please
___ 6. PERPETUALLY   F. Quality of being pleasant & easy to speak with
___ 7. CONJUGAL   G. Money given to support the clergy
___ 8. ASCERTAINING   H. Credit
___ 9. TACITURN   I. Motivated by money or material goods
___10. INSOLENT   J. Postpone
___11. CIRCUMSPECTION   K. Prudence
___12. ALACRITY   L. Improperly bold or forward
___13. SANGUINE   M. Not talkative
___14. IMPLACABLE   N. Totally occupied
___15. SUPERCILIOUS   O. Continually; constantly
___16. BREVITY   P. Cheerful willingness
___17. MERCENARY   Q. Finding out; discovering
___18. AFFABILITY   R. Shortness; quality of being short in duration
___19. ENGROSSED   S. Grumbling; complaining
___20. PROFLIGATE   T. Cheerfully confident; optimistic
___21. QUERULOUS   U. Wasteful; extravagant
___22. IMPERTINENT   V. Abusive language
___23. VALID   W. Insulting; disrespectful; rude
___24. RECTITUDE   X. Relating to marriage
___25. TACIT   Y. Empty

Pride & Prejudice Vocabulary Matching 3 Answer Key

V - 1.	INVECTIVES	A. Haughty; disdainful
J - 2.	DEFER	B. Implied by action
Y - 3.	VOID	C. Legal and binding
H - 4.	IMPUTE	D. Moral uprightness
G - 5.	TITHES	E. Impossible to appease or please
O - 6.	PERPETUALLY	F. Quality of being pleasant & easy to speak with
X - 7.	CONJUGAL	G. Money given to support the clergy
Q - 8.	ASCERTAINING	H. Credit
M - 9.	TACITURN	I. Motivated by money or material goods
W - 10.	INSOLENT	J. Postpone
K - 11.	CIRCUMSPECTION	K. Prudence
P - 12.	ALACRITY	L. Improperly bold or forward
T - 13.	SANGUINE	M. Not talkative
E - 14.	IMPLACABLE	N. Totally occupied
A - 15.	SUPERCILIOUS	O. Continually; constantly
R - 16.	BREVITY	P. Cheerful willingness
I - 17.	MERCENARY	Q. Finding out; discovering
F - 18.	AFFABILITY	R. Shortness; quality of being short in duration
N - 19.	ENGROSSED	S. Grumbling; complaining
U - 20.	PROFLIGATE	T. Cheerfully confident; optimistic
S - 21.	QUERULOUS	U. Wasteful; extravagant
L - 22.	IMPERTINENT	V. Abusive language
C - 23.	VALID	W. Insulting; disrespectful; rude
D - 24.	RECTITUDE	X. Relating to marriage
B - 25.	TACIT	Y. Empty

Copyrighted

Pride & Prejudice Vocabulary Matching 4

___ 1. DESTITUTE   A. Unclear; not well defined
___ 2. INSOLENT   B. Insulting; disrespectful; rude
___ 3. IMPUTE   C. Intense joy
___ 4. INJUNCTIONS   D. Impulsive change of mind
___ 5. TRACTABLE   E. Cheerfully confident; optimistic
___ 6. CONJECTURE   F. Pretentious; pompous
___ 7. AFFABILITY   G. Repaid
___ 8. ASCERTAINING   H. Do a favor or service for
___ 9. OBLIGE   I. Lacking; poor
___10. VAGUE   J. Money given to support the clergy
___11. REQUITED   K. Improperly bold or forward
___12. PECUNIARY   L. Thicket of small trees
___13. ECSTASY   M. Tending to delay
___14. COPSE   N. Meticulous; concerned with details; difficult to please
___15. IMPERTINENT   O. Credit
___16. OSTENTATIOUS   P. Of little significance
___17. FASTIDIOUS   Q. Fashion; popularity
___18. VOGUE   R. Manageable; easily handled
___19. SANGUINE   S. Guess
___20. TITHES   T. Commands; orders
___21. DILATORY   U. Quality of being pleasant & easy to speak with
___22. TRIFLING   V. Relating to money
___23. REPINE   W. Continually; constantly
___24. PERPETUALLY   X. Finding out; discovering
___25. CAPRICE   Y. To be discontented or in low spirits

Pride & Prejudice Vocabulary Matching 4 Answer Key

I - 1. DESTITUTE		A. Unclear; not well defined
B - 2. INSOLENT		B. Insulting; disrespectful; rude
O - 3. IMPUTE		C. Intense joy
T - 4. INJUNCTIONS		D. Impulsive change of mind
R - 5. TRACTABLE		E. Cheerfully confident; optimistic
S - 6. CONJECTURE		F. Pretentious; pompous
U - 7. AFFABILITY		G. Repaid
X - 8. ASCERTAINING		H. Do a favor or service for
H - 9. OBLIGE		I. Lacking; poor
A - 10. VAGUE		J. Money given to support the clergy
G - 11. REQUITED		K. Improperly bold or forward
V - 12. PECUNIARY		L. Thicket of small trees
C - 13. ECSTASY		M. Tending to delay
L - 14. COPSE		N. Meticulous; concerned with details; difficult to please
K - 15. IMPERTINENT		O. Credit
F - 16. OSTENTATIOUS		P. Of little significance
N - 17. FASTIDIOUS		Q. Fashion; popularity
Q - 18. VOGUE		R. Manageable; easily handled
E - 19. SANGUINE		S. Guess
J - 20. TITHES		T. Commands; orders
M - 21. DILATORY		U. Quality of being pleasant & easy to speak with
P - 22. TRIFLING		V. Relating to money
Y - 23. REPINE		W. Continually; constantly
W - 24. PERPETUALLY		X. Finding out; discovering
D - 25. CAPRICE		Y. To be discontented or in low spirits

Pride & Prejudice Vocabulary Magic Squares 1

Match the definition with the vocabulary word. Put your answers in the magic squares below. When your answers are correct, all columns and rows will add to the same number.

A. ENTREATIES
B. OBLIGE
C. ASPIRE
D. REQUITED
E. EFFUSION
F. APPROBATION
G. PLIANCY
H. ALACRITY
I. IMPLACABLE
J. DEFER
K. IMPUTE
L. VOGUE
M. COGENT
N. TRACTABLE
O. VAGUE
P. MERCENARY

1. Approval
2. Impossible to appease or please
3. Unclear; not well defined
4. Repaid
5. Convincing
6. Do a favor or service for
7. Cheerful willingness
8. Credit
9. Desire; have an ambition or goal
10. Motivated by money or material goods
11. Postpone
12. Unrestrained outpouring of speech
13. Fashion; popularity
14. Flexibility
15. Pleas
16. Manageable; easily handled

A=	B=	C=	D=
E=	F=	G=	H=
I=	J=	K=	L=
M=	N=	O=	P=

Pride & Prejudice Vocabulary Magic Squares 1 Answer Key

Match the definition with the vocabulary word. Put your answers in the magic squares below. When your answers are correct, all columns and rows will add to the same number.

A. ENTREATIES
B. OBLIGE
C. ASPIRE
D. REQUITED
E. EFFUSION
F. APPROBATION
G. PLIANCY
H. ALACRITY
I. IMPLACABLE
J. DEFER
K. IMPUTE
L. VOGUE
M. COGENT
N. TRACTABLE
O. VAGUE
P. MERCENARY

1. Approval
2. Impossible to appease or please
3. Unclear; not well defined
4. Repaid
5. Convincing
6. Do a favor or service for
7. Cheerful willingness
8. Credit
9. Desire; have an ambition or goal
10. Motivated by money or material goods
11. Postpone
12. Unrestrained outpouring of speech
13. Fashion; popularity
14. Flexibility
15. Pleas
16. Manageable; easily handled

A=15	B=6	C=9	D=4
E=12	F=1	G=14	H=7
I=2	J=11	K=8	L=13
M=5	N=16	O=3	P=10

Pride & Prejudice Vocabulary Magic Squares 2

Match the definition with the vocabulary word. Put your answers in the magic squares below. When your answers are correct, all columns and rows will add to the same number.

A. FASTIDIOUS
B. BREVITY
C. AFFINITY
D. INSOLENT
E. OMEN
F. TITHES
G. PECUNIARY
H. TACITURN
I. APPROBATION
J. AFFABILITY
K. CAPRICE
L. ASCERTAINING
M. IMPERTINENT
N. TRIFLING
O. INJUNCTIONS
P. VALID

1. Commands; orders
2. Insulting; disrespectful; rude
3. Quality of being pleasant & easy to speak with
4. A sign of the future
5. Approval
6. Money given to support the clergy
7. Legal and binding
8. Natural attraction to
9. Not talkative
10. Impulsive change of mind
11. Meticulous; concerned with details; difficult to please
12. Of little significance
13. Shortness; quality of being short in duration
14. Improperly bold or forward
15. Relating to money
16. Finding out; discovering

A=	B=	C=	D=
E=	F=	G=	H=
I=	J=	K=	L=
M=	N=	O=	P=

Pride & Prejudice Vocabulary Magic Squares 2 Answer Key

Match the definition with the vocabulary word. Put your answers in the magic squares below. When your answers are correct, all columns and rows will add to the same number.

A. FASTIDIOUS
B. BREVITY
C. AFFINITY
D. INSOLENT
E. OMEN
F. TITHES
G. PECUNIARY
H. TACITURN
I. APPROBATION
J. AFFABILITY
K. CAPRICE
L. ASCERTAINING
M. IMPERTINENT
N. TRIFLING
O. INJUNCTIONS
P. VALID

1. Commands; orders
2. Insulting; disrespectful; rude
3. Quality of being pleasant & easy to speak with
4. A sign of the future
5. Approval
6. Money given to support the clergy
7. Legal and binding
8. Natural attraction to
9. Not talkative
10. Impulsive change of mind
11. Meticulous; concerned with details; difficult to please
12. Of little significance
13. Shortness; quality of being short in duration
14. Improperly bold or forward
15. Relating to money
16. Finding out; discovering

A=11	B=13	C=8	D=2
E=4	F=6	G=15	H=9
I=5	J=3	K=10	L=16
M=14	N=12	O=1	P=7

Pride & Prejudice Vocabulary Magic Squares 3

Match the definition with the vocabulary word. Put your answers in the magic squares below. When your answers are correct, all columns and rows will add to the same number.

A. PECUNIARY
B. AFFABILITY
C. INCUMBENT
D. EFFUSION
E. QUERULOUS
F. VAGUE
G. DIMINUTION
H. INVECTIVES
I. PURSUED
J. VALID
K. PROFLIGATE
L. TRACTABLE
M. IMPUTE
N. DERISION
O. BREVITY
P. OMEN

1. Abusive language
2. Relating to money
3. Quality of being pleasant & easy to speak with
4. Reduction
5. Legal and binding
6. Shortness; quality of being short in duration
7. A sign of the future
8. Advanced; chased after
9. Wasteful; extravagant
10. Ridicule
11. Credit
12. Manageable; easily handled
13. Grumbling; complaining
14. Unrestrained outpouring of speech
15. Imposed as a duty or obligation
16. Unclear; not well defined

A=	B=	C=	D=
E=	F=	G=	H=
I=	J=	K=	L=
M=	N=	O=	P=

Pride & Prejudice Vocabulary Magic Squares 3 Answer Key

Match the definition with the vocabulary word. Put your answers in the magic squares below. When your answers are correct, all columns and rows will add to the same number.

A. PECUNIARY
B. AFFABILITY
C. INCUMBENT
D. EFFUSION
E. QUERULOUS
F. VAGUE
G. DIMINUTION
H. INVECTIVES
I. PURSUED
J. VALID
K. PROFLIGATE
L. TRACTABLE
M. IMPUTE
N. DERISION
O. BREVITY
P. OMEN

1. Abusive language
2. Relating to money
3. Quality of being pleasant & easy to speak with
4. Reduction
5. Legal and binding
6. Shortness; quality of being short in duration
7. A sign of the future
8. Advanced; chased after
9. Wasteful; extravagant
10. Ridicule
11. Credit
12. Manageable; easily handled
13. Grumbling; complaining
14. Unrestrained outpouring of speech
15. Imposed as a duty or obligation
16. Unclear; not well defined

A=2	B=3	C=15	D=14
E=13	F=16	G=4	H=1
I=8	J=5	K=9	L=12
M=11	N=10	O=6	P=7

Pride & Prejudice Vocabulary Magic Squares 4

Match the definition with the vocabulary word. Put your answers in the magic squares below. When your answers are correct, all columns and rows will add to the same number.

A. OSTENTATIOUS
B. IMPUTE
C. PROPITIOUS
D. ENTREATIES
E. MERCENARY
F. INVECTIVES
G. VOLUBILITY
H. AFFABILITY
I. BREVITY
J. EFFICACY
K. FASTIDIOUS
L. PURSUED
M. TACITURN
N. AFFINITY
O. REQUITED
P. COGENT

1. Not talkative
2. Abusive language
3. Quality of being pleasant & easy to speak with
4. Repaid
5. Advanced; chased after
6. Favorable
7. Pretentious; pompous
8. Effectiveness
9. Meticulous; concerned with details; difficult to please
10. Pleas
11. Credit
12. Shortness; quality of being short in duration
13. Natural attraction to
14. Motivated by money or material goods
15. Fluency of speech
16. Convincing

A=	B=	C=	D=
E=	F=	G=	H=
I=	J=	K=	L=
M=	N=	O=	P=

Pride & Prejudice Vocabulary Magic Squares 4 Answer Key

Match the definition with the vocabulary word. Put your answers in the magic squares below. When your answers are correct, all columns and rows will add to the same number.

A. OSTENTATIOUS
B. IMPUTE
C. PROPITIOUS
D. ENTREATIES
E. MERCENARY
F. INVECTIVES
G. VOLUBILITY
H. AFFABILITY
I. BREVITY
J. EFFICACY
K. FASTIDIOUS
L. PURSUED
M. TACITURN
N. AFFINITY
O. REQUITED
P. COGENT

1. Not talkative
2. Abusive language
3. Quality of being pleasant & easy to speak with
4. Repaid
5. Advanced; chased after
6. Favorable
7. Pretentious; pompous
8. Effectiveness
9. Meticulous; concerned with details; difficult to please
10. Pleas
11. Credit
12. Shortness; quality of being short in duration
13. Natural attraction to
14. Motivated by money or material goods
15. Fluency of speech
16. Convincing

A=7	B=11	C=6	D=10
E=14	F=2	G=15	H=3
I=12	J=8	K=9	L=5
M=1	N=13	O=4	P=16

Pride & Prejudice Vocabulary Word Search 1

Words are placed backwards, forward, diagonally, up and down. Clues listed below can help you find the words. Circle the hidden vocabulary words in the maze.

```
B I Y Y A T R O M E R C E N A R Y E T S
C N T S S D I Q B P A N E G Y R I C C Z
V C I U P G W T D E L G E T P E W S H D
F U R P I R Z N H D I T Z K L N Q T E G
O M C E R J O Y H E U S N B I I F A L W
Y B A R E I W T G T S K A C A P R S P K
G E L C S N H J I C W A J N N E S Y U D
W N A I N O I T C E P S M U C R I C R Q
G T R L G S S N A Q S C A N Y E L E C R
C E F I H E V E R C J E I G V V F Y S Q
D F P O D V A G U E I R N A A E O Y P P
I A A U L O L O Z F N T J P D C V G N Q
L C F S Y I I C P F S A U P L N I Z U K
A Q A F T D D G M U O I N R E E Q T Z E
T S J P I I J W D S L N C O N N U P Y B
O J I G R N D Y T I E I T B C G E U T Y
R O M E N I I I V O N N I A O R R R I K
Y W P V N Z C T O N T G O T P O U S C M
W S U P Y A P E Y U B J N I S S L U A K
L F T L T M C Z Z L S T S O E S O E R Z
Q Q E F F I C A C Y Y K P N H E U D E S
B R E V I T Y T R I F L I N G D S P V P
```

A sign of the future (4)
Advanced; chased after (7)
Approval (11)
Cheerful willingness (8)
Commands; orders (11)
Convincing (6)
Credit (6)
Desire for the possessions of others (4)
Desire; have an ambition or goal (6)
Do a favor or service for (6)
Effectiveness (8)
Empty (4)
Fashion; popularity (5)
Finding out; discovering (12)
Flexibility (7)
Gesture of deference or homage (9)
Grumbling; complaining (9)
Haughty; disdainful (12)
Hesitate as a result of conscience (7)
Implied by action (5)
Imposed as a duty or obligation (9)
Impulsive change of mind (7)
Insulting; disrespectful; rude (8)

Intense joy (7)
Judgement; wisdom (8)
Lacking; poor (9)
Legal and binding (5)
Meticulous; concerned with details; difficult to please (10)
Money given to support the clergy (6)
Motivated by money or material goods (9)
Natural attraction to (8)
Not talkative (8)
Of little significance (8)
Postpone (5)
Praise; compliment (9)
Prudence (14)
Ridicule (8)
Shortness; quality of being short in duration (7)
Tending to delay (8)
Thicket of small trees (5)
To be discontented or in low spirits (6)
Totally occupied (9)
Truthfulness (8)
Unclear; not well defined (5)
Unrestrained outpouring of speech (8)

Pride & Prejudice Vocabulary Word Search 1 Answer Key

Words are placed backwards, forward, diagonally, up and down. Clues listed below can help you find the words. Circle the hidden vocabulary words in the maze.

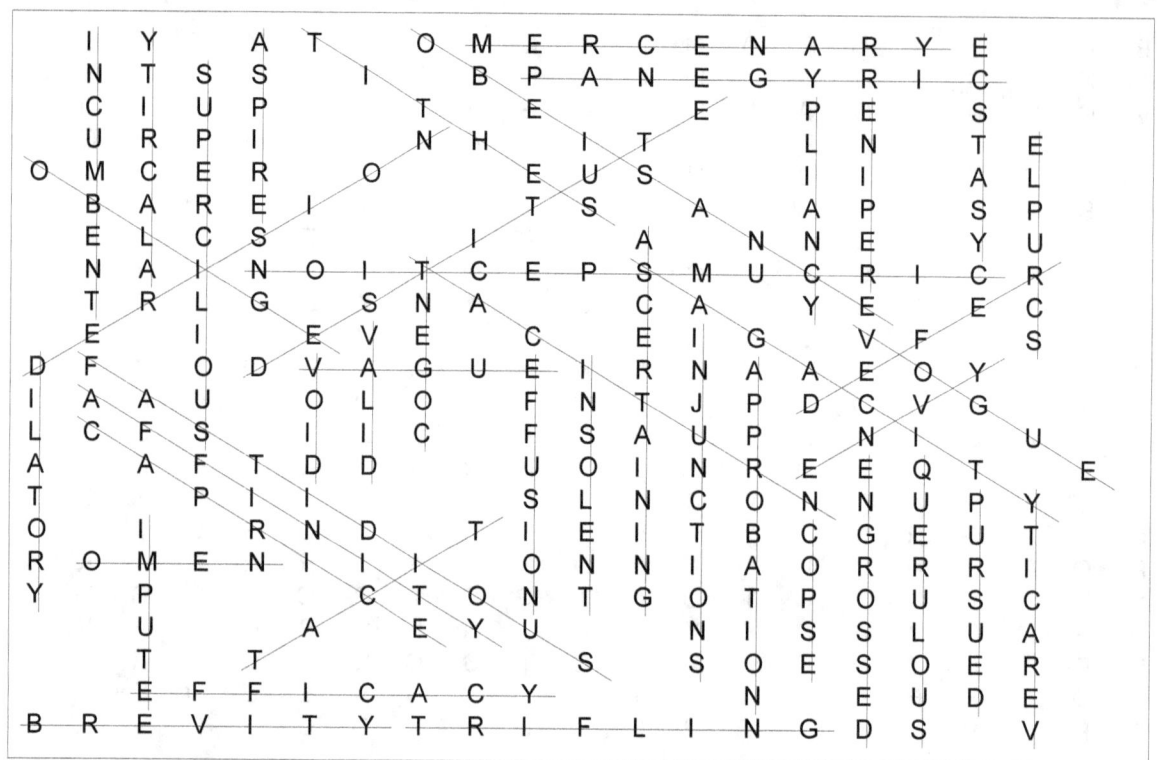

A sign of the future (4)
Advanced; chased after (7)
Approval (11)
Cheerful willingness (8)
Commands; orders (11)
Convincing (6)
Credit (6)
Desire for the possessions of others (4)
Desire; have an ambition or goal (6)
Do a favor or service for (6)
Effectiveness (8)
Empty (4)
Fashion; popularity (5)
Finding out; discovering (12)
Flexibility (7)
Gesture of deference or homage (9)
Grumbling; complaining (9)
Haughty; disdainful (12)
Hesitate as a result of conscience (7)
Implied by action (5)
Imposed as a duty or obligation (9)
Impulsive change of mind (7)
Insulting; disrespectful; rude (8)

Intense joy (7)
Judgement; wisdom (8)
Lacking; poor (9)
Legal and binding (5)
Meticulous; concerned with details; difficult to please (10)
Money given to support the clergy (6)
Motivated by money or material goods (9)
Natural attraction to (8)
Not talkative (8)
Of little significance (8)
Postpone (5)
Praise; compliment (9)
Prudence (14)
Ridicule (8)
Shortness; quality of being short in duration (7)
Tending to delay (8)
Thicket of small trees (5)
To be discontented or in low spirits (6)
Totally occupied (9)
Truthfulness (8)
Unclear; not well defined (5)
Unrestrained outpouring of speech (8)

Pride & Prejudice Vocabulary Word Search 2

Words are placed backwards, forward, diagonally, up and down. Clues listed below can help you find the words. Circle the hidden vocabulary words in the maze.

```
R A D R C M M V I N J U N C T I O N S J
E U I E P I V E E E L B A C A L P M I K
P G L C D E R N R R G N I L F I R T L B
I M A T M Z C C S C A P A N E G Y R I C
N E T I C A T U U K E C N A S I E B O P
E N O T M O G K N M R N I Y M J H F R G
I T R U K Q G C D I S V A T F L T O C V
M E Y D C Y L E T T A P H R Y F F M O D
P D B E W A U Y N Z N R E S Y L D V N K
E P E B L S P X G T G F Y C I M W P J W
R P J S R H E R N D U D R G T D C L U Y
T M W U T H C T I D I P A J Y I B I G K
I D P X Z I S Y N C N T F S A M O A A S
N S E H T I T S I H E F F U S I O N L X
E U G O V I A U A M S Y P O P N B C I F
N Z K R N G S M T V P D N I I U R Y N W
T J T I A K Y D R E O V G T R T E V S S
N T F C H V B B E X C I G I E I V A O X
D F I Q N X Y N C F L X D P S O I L L G
A T B E N G R O S S E D D O X N T I E N
Y O M E N E U G A V T R J N Q Y D N M
T A C I T U R N H M E T U P M I X D T P
```

A sign of the future (4)
Added (9)
Advanced; chased after (7)
Cheerful willingness (8)
Cheerfully confident; optimistic (8)
Commands; orders (11)
Convincing (6)
Credit (6)
Desire for the possessions of others (4)
Desire; have an ambition or goal (6)
Empty (4)
Fashion; popularity (5)
Favorable (10)
Finding out; discovering (12)
Flexibility (7)
Gesture of deference or homage (9)
Implied by action (5)
Impossible to appease or please (10)
Improperly bold or forward (11)
Impulsive change of mind (7)
Insulting; disrespectful; rude (8)
Intense joy (7)
Judgement; wisdom (8)

Lacking; poor (9)
Legal and binding (5)
Money given to support the clergy (6)
Moral uprightness (9)
Motivated by money or material goods (9)
Natural attraction to (8)
Not talkative (8)
Of little significance (8)
Postpone (5)
Praise; compliment (9)
Prudence (14)
Reduction (10)
Relating to marriage (8)
Relating to money (9)
Shortness; quality of being short in duration (7)
Tending to delay (8)
Thicket of small trees (5)
To be discontented or in low spirits (6)
Totally occupied (9)
Truthfulness (8)
Unclear; not well defined (5)
Unrestrained outpouring of speech (8)
Wasteful; extravagant (10)

Pride & Prejudice Vocabulary Word Search 2 Answer Key

Words are placed backwards, forward, diagonally, up and down. Clues listed below can help you find the words. Circle the hidden vocabulary words in the maze.

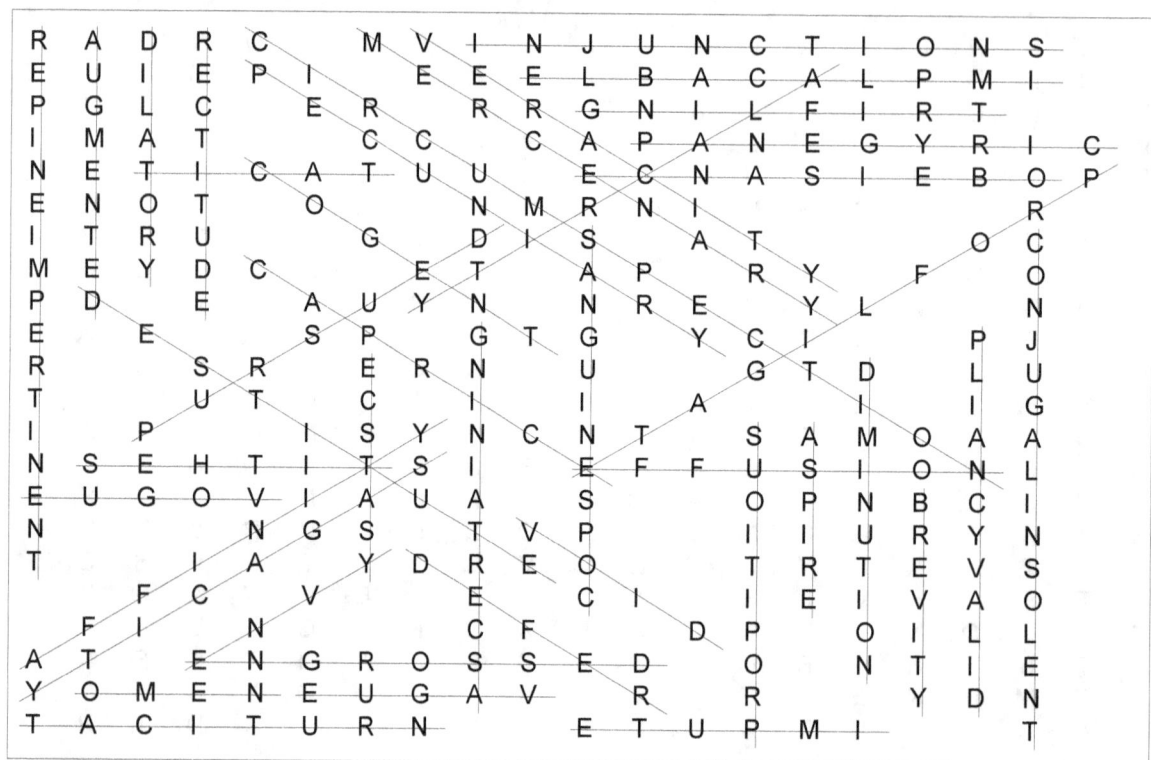

A sign of the future (4)
Added (9)
Advanced; chased after (7)
Cheerful willingness (8)
Cheerfully confident; optimistic (8)
Commands; orders (11)
Convincing (6)
Credit (6)
Desire for the possessions of others (4)
Desire; have an ambition or goal (6)
Empty (4)
Fashion; popularity (5)
Favorable (10)
Finding out; discovering (12)
Flexibility (7)
Gesture of deference or homage (9)
Implied by action (5)
Impossible to appease or please (10)
Improperly bold or forward (11)
Impulsive change of mind (7)
Insulting; disrespectful; rude (8)
Intense joy (7)
Judgement; wisdom (8)

Lacking; poor (9)
Legal and binding (5)
Money given to support the clergy (6)
Moral uprightness (9)
Motivated by money or material goods (9)
Natural attraction to (8)
Not talkative (8)
Of little significance (8)
Postpone (5)
Praise; compliment (9)
Prudence (14)
Reduction (10)
Relating to marriage (8)
Relating to money (9)
Shortness; quality of being short in duration (7)
Tending to delay (8)
Thicket of small trees (5)
To be discontented or in low spirits (6)
Totally occupied (9)
Truthfulness (8)
Unclear; not well defined (5)
Unrestrained outpouring of speech (8)
Wasteful; extravagant (10)

Pride & Prejudice Vocabulary Word Search 3

Words are placed backwards, forward, diagonally, up and down. Words listed below are included in the maze. Circle the hidden vocabulary words in the maze.

```
E G I L B O S A N G U I N E S S Z X A R
N Y Y P P I N S O L E N T U U E F P B B
G F C D Z L N P F N H H O O L Y P Z D S
R I N V E C T I V E S L I B T R F S I L
O T A C I T U R N D U T A I O S E D L H
S R I Y D V P E L R A C N B C H J L A B
S V L R P U J K E T A I A R T B X L T V
E A P S R C S U N L F T U I L A S Q O W
D G B S P O Q E P F I P T P S Y C G R L
M U U M H P T M A O L C C U D P U I Y F
F E F F U S I O N E M O O B R E V I T Y
D T R M O E A J B Q M I N G B C F O F Y
C U D C Q P D G K E T W J H E U Q E I L
O T E E E P A C A I I Z U D B N Y C R D
N I R N T N S N P C D S G W V I T S E H
J T I V U Z A O E E I X A Y C A D T P X
E S S Y P W R R T G F T L N T R P A I Z
C E I H M P G I Y B Y L Y X C Y B S N D
T D O Q I R U F C A P R I C E E S Y E R
U R N S J Q N O I T U N I M I D S C K R
R I M P E R T I N E N T Y C A C I F F E
E C I R C U M S P E C T I O N V A L I D
```

AFFINITY	DESTITUTE	INVECTIVES	REPINE
APPROBATION	DILATORY	MERCENARY	REQUITED
ASPIRE	DIMINUTION	OBEISANCE	SAGACITY
BREVITY	ECSTASY	OBLIGE	SANGUINE
CAPRICE	EFFICACY	OMEN	SCRUPLE
CIRCUMSPECTION	EFFUSION	OSTENTATIOUS	TACIT
COGENT	ENGROSSED	PANEGYRIC	TACITURN
CONJECTURE	ENVY	PECUNIARY	TITHES
CONJUGAL	IMPERTINENT	PLIANCY	VAGUE
COPSE	IMPLACABLE	PROPITIOUS	VALID
DEFER	IMPUTE	PURSUED	VOGUE
DERISION	INSOLENT	QUERULOUS	VOID

Pride & Prejudice Vocabulary Word Search 3 Answer Key

Words are placed backwards, forward, diagonally, up and down. Words listed below are included in the maze. Circle the hidden vocabulary words in the maze.

AFFINITY	DESTITUTE	INVECTIVES	REPINE
APPROBATION	DILATORY	MERCENARY	REQUITED
ASPIRE	DIMINUTION	OBEISANCE	SAGACITY
BREVITY	ECSTASY	OBLIGE	SANGUINE
CAPRICE	EFFICACY	OMEN	SCRUPLE
CIRCUMSPECTION	EFFUSION	OSTENTATIOUS	TACIT
COGENT	ENGROSSED	PANEGYRIC	TACITURN
CONJECTURE	ENVY	PECUNIARY	TITHES
CONJUGAL	IMPERTINENT	PLIANCY	VAGUE
COPSE	IMPLACABLE	PROPITIOUS	VALID
DEFER	IMPUTE	PURSUED	VOGUE
DERISION	INSOLENT	QUERULOUS	VOID

Pride & Prejudice Vocabulary Word Search 4

Words are placed backwards, forward, diagonally, up and down. Words listed below are included in the maze. Circle the hidden vocabulary words in the maze.

```
P E R P E T U A L L Y R O T A L I D D M
R K B I R V B T R A C T A B L E K E E K
O Z C M U E R D E S T I T U T E U Z T L
F V N P T R E O M P A R K L E S D Y N C
L S H R C A V S T A C I T U R N T H E V
I A S U E C I T I I I J T U K I V F M K
G G A D J I T E E N T V P Q R Z F Y G K
A A N E N T Y N L C V R R C N I S D U T
T C G N O Y V T P U K E A X C C U E A W
E I U C C C M A U M N L C A Y D O F P D
P T I E R O F T R B A H C T B T L E A N
C Y N W G G C I C E V Y O Z I S U R N D
F O E V D E F O S N Q G B F U V R I E T
R N N X N N E U K T D U E O H C E P G V
E H T J B T C S F A S T I D I O U S Y N
C P Y F U K S C D R H T S T M P Q A R V
T N G P C G T F A E I O A E E C R V I R
I I M Y C N A I L P L B N V C D E A C K
T I T O F Y S L O I R L C D A U V G V S
U B P H L R Y R N N Y I E X G L M U G P
D S R P E F P M F E Q G C O Y G I E T Z
E G B I N S O L E N T E V E V O I D G Z
```

ALACRITY	DESTITUTE	INVECTIVES	PURSUED	TITHES
ASPIRE	DILATORY	OBEISANCE	QUERULOUS	TRACTABLE
AUGMENTED	ECSTASY	OBLIGE	RECTITUDE	VAGUE
BREVITY	EFFICACY	OMEN	REPINE	VALID
CAPRICE	ENVY	OSTENTATIOUS	REQUITED	VERACITY
COGENT	FASTIDIOUS	PANEGYRIC	SAGACITY	VOGUE
CONJECTURE	IMPRUDENCE	PERPETUALLY	SANGUINE	VOID
CONJUGAL	IMPUTE	PLIANCY	SCRUPLE	
COPSE	INCUMBENT	PROFLIGATE	TACIT	
DEFER	INSOLENT	PROPITIOUS	TACITURN	

Pride & Prejudice Vocabulary Word Search 4 Answer Key

Words are placed backwards, forward, diagonally, up and down. Words listed below are included in the maze. Circle the hidden vocabulary words in the maze.

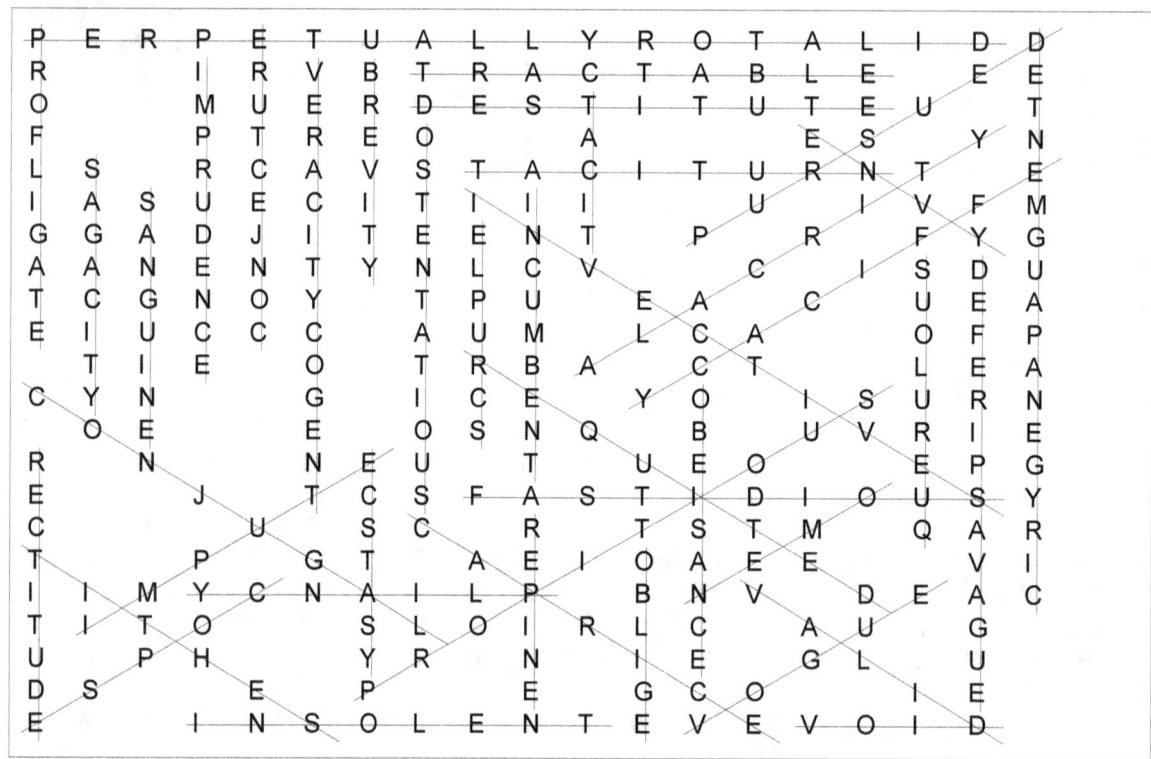

ALACRITY	DESTITUTE	INVECTIVES	PURSUED	TITHES
ASPIRE	DILATORY	OBEISANCE	QUERULOUS	TRACTABLE
AUGMENTED	ECSTASY	OBLIGE	RECTITUDE	VAGUE
BREVITY	EFFICACY	OMEN	REPINE	VALID
CAPRICE	ENVY	OSTENTATIOUS	REQUITED	VERACITY
COGENT	FASTIDIOUS	PANEGYRIC	SAGACITY	VOGUE
CONJECTURE	IMPRUDENCE	PERPETUALLY	SANGUINE	VOID
CONJUGAL	IMPUTE	PLIANCY	SCRUPLE	
COPSE	INCUMBENT	PROFLIGATE	TACIT	
DEFER	INSOLENT	PROPITIOUS	TACITURN	

Pride & Prejudice Vocabulary Crossword 1

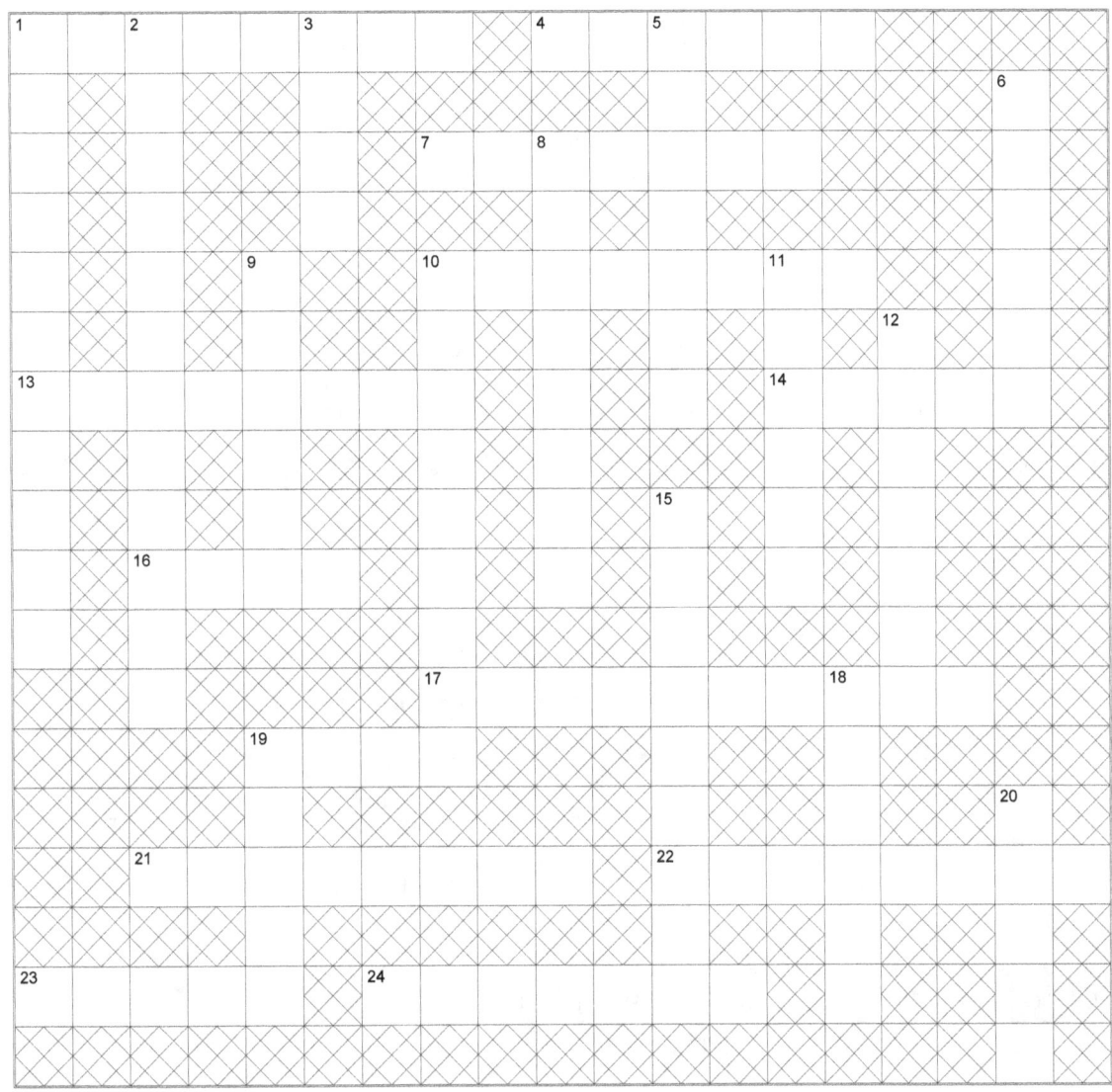

Across
1. Insulting; disrespectful; rude
4. To be discontented or in low spirits
7. Shortness; quality of being short in duration
10. Natural attraction to
13. Of little significance
14. Implied by action
16. A sign of the future
17. Pleas
19. Empty
21. Judgement; wisdom
22. Repaid
23. Thicket of small trees
24. Impulsive change of mind

Down
1. Commands; orders
2. Haughty; disdainful
3. Desire for the possessions of others
5. Flexibility
6. Convincing
8. Unrestrained outpouring of speech
9. Do a favor or service for
10. Added
11. Money given to support the clergy
12. Hesitate as a result of conscience
15. Praise; compliment
18. Credit
19. Fashion; popularity
20. Postpone

Pride & Prejudice Vocabulary Crossword 1 Answer Key

	1 I	2 N	S	O	L	3 E	N	T		4 R	5 E	P	I	N	E		
	N		U			N					L						6 C
	J		P			V		7 B	8 R	E	V	I	T	Y			O
	U		E			Y			F			A					G
	N		R		9 O		10 A	F	F	I	N	I	11 T	Y			E
	C		C		B		U		U			C		I		12 S		N
13 T	R	I	F	L	I	N	G		S			Y		14 T	A	C	I	T
	I		L		I		M		I					H		R		
	O		I		G		E		O		15 P			E		U		
	N		16 O	M	E	N		N			A			S		P		
	S		U					T			N					L		
			S				17 E	N	T	R	E	A	18 T	I	E	S		
					19 V	O	I	D			G		M					
					O						Y		P				20 D	
			21 S	A	G	A	C	I	T	Y			22 R	E	Q	U	I	T	E	D
					U								I				T		F	
	23 C	O	P	S	E		24 C	A	P	R	I	C	E				T		E	
																			R	

Across
1. Insulting; disrespectful; rude
4. To be discontented or in low spirits
7. Shortness; quality of being short in duration
10. Natural attraction to
13. Of little significance
14. Implied by action
16. A sign of the future
17. Pleas
19. Empty
21. Judgement; wisdom
22. Repaid
23. Thicket of small trees
24. Impulsive change of mind

Down
1. Commands; orders
2. Haughty; disdainful
3. Desire for the possessions of others
5. Flexibility
6. Convincing
8. Unrestrained outpouring of speech
9. Do a favor or service for
10. Added
11. Money given to support the clergy
12. Hesitate as a result of conscience
15. Praise; compliment
18. Credit
19. Fashion; popularity
20. Postpone

Pride & Prejudice Vocabulary Crossword 2

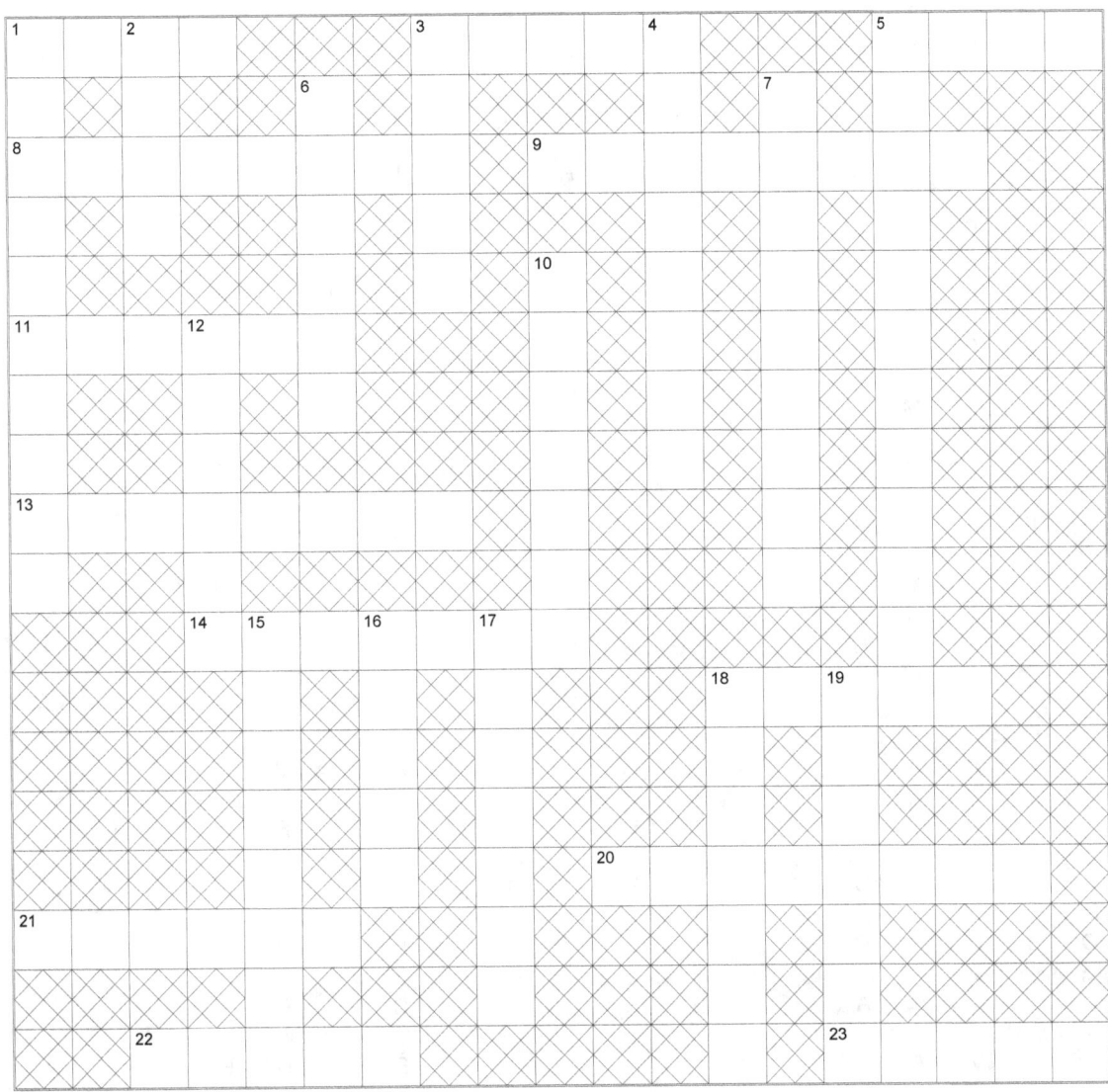

Across
1. Desire for the possessions of others
3. Fashion; popularity
5. A sign of the future
8. Of little significance
9. Natural attraction to
11. Desire; have an ambition or goal
13. Unrestrained outpouring of speech
14. Intense joy
18. Thicket of small trees
20. Ridicule
21. Do a favor or service for
22. Legal and binding
23. Postpone

Down
1. Pleas
2. Empty
3. Unclear; not well defined
4. Effectiveness
5. Pretentious; pompous
6. Money given to support the clergy
7. Imposed as a duty or obligation
10. Shortness; quality of being short in duration
12. Credit
15. Relating to marriage
16. Implied by action
17. Hesitate as a result of conscience
18. Impulsive change of mind
19. Advanced; chased after

Pride & Prejudice Vocabulary Crossword 2 Answer Key

Across
1. Desire for the possessions of others
3. Fashion; popularity
5. A sign of the future
8. Of little significance
9. Natural attraction to
11. Desire; have an ambition or goal
13. Unrestrained outpouring of speech
14. Intense joy
18. Thicket of small trees
20. Ridicule
21. Do a favor or service for
22. Legal and binding
23. Postpone

Down
1. Pleas
2. Empty
3. Unclear; not well defined
4. Effectiveness
5. Pretentious; pompous
6. Money given to support the clergy
7. Imposed as a duty or obligation
10. Shortness; quality of being short in duration
12. Credit
15. Relating to marriage
16. Implied by action
17. Hesitate as a result of conscience
18. Impulsive change of mind
19. Advanced; chased after

Pride & Prejudice Vocabulary Crossword 3

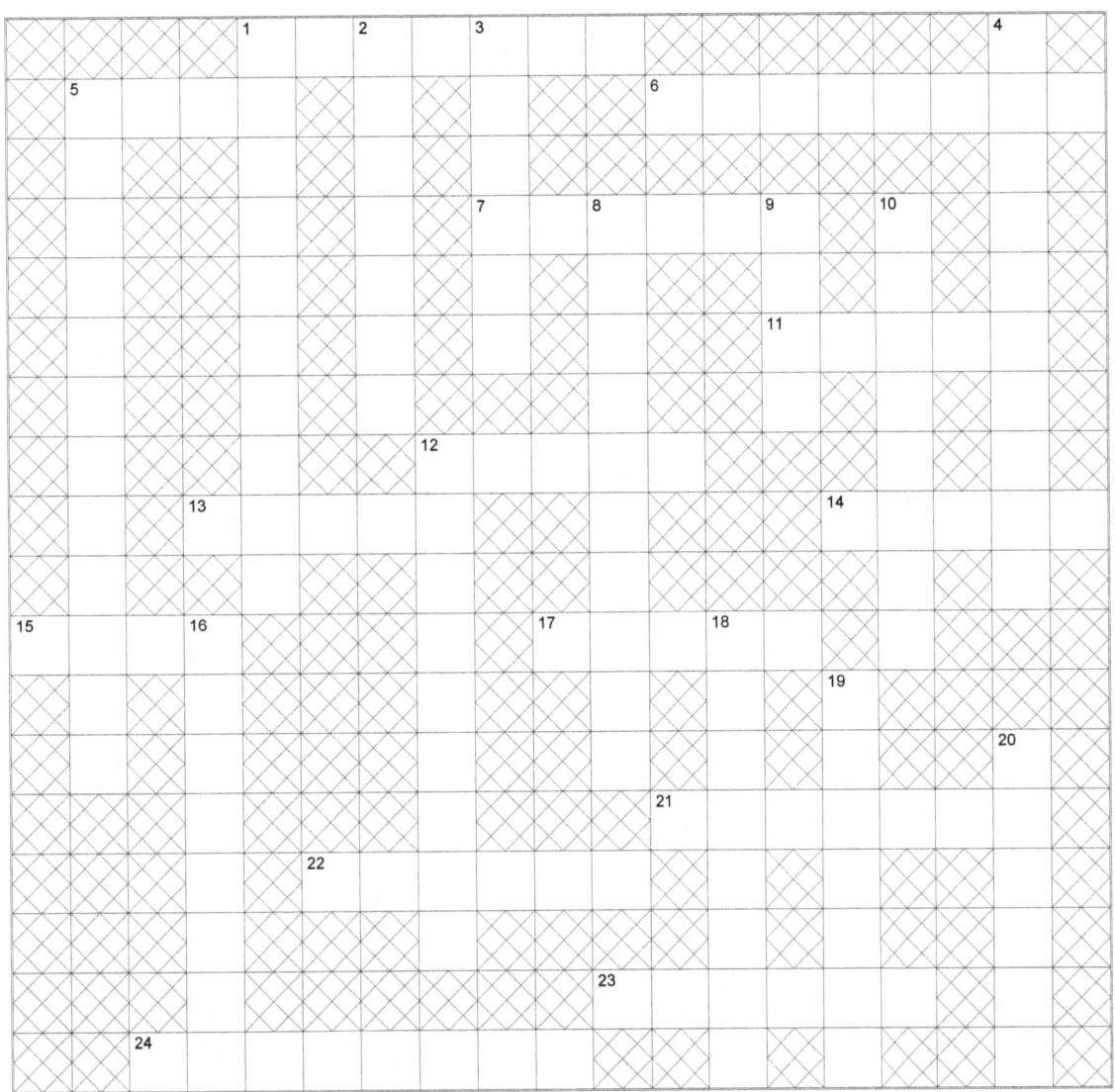

Across
1. Intense joy
5. A sign of the future
6. Relating to marriage
7. Credit
11. Legal and binding
12. Implied by action
13. Postpone
14. Fashion; popularity
15. Empty
17. Thicket of small trees
21. Impulsive change of mind
22. Do a favor or service for
23. Money given to support the clergy
24. Insulting; disrespectful; rude

Down
1. Pleas
2. Hesitate as a result of conscience
3. Desire; have an ambition or goal
4. Meticulous; concerned with details; difficult to please
5. Pretentious; pompous
8. Favorable
9. Desire for the possessions of others
10. Tending to delay
12. Manageable; easily handled
16. Ridicule
18. Judgement; wisdom
19. Advanced; chased after
20. To be discontented or in low spirits

Pride & Prejudice Vocabulary Crossword 3 Answer Key

Across
1. Intense joy
5. A sign of the future
6. Relating to marriage
7. Credit
11. Legal and binding
12. Implied by action
13. Postpone
14. Fashion; popularity
15. Empty
17. Thicket of small trees
21. Impulsive change of mind
22. Do a favor or service for
23. Money given to support the clergy
24. Insulting; disrespectful; rude

Down
1. Pleas
2. Hesitate as a result of conscience
3. Desire; have an ambition or goal
4. Meticulous; concerned with details; difficult to please
5. Pretentious; pompous
8. Favorable
9. Desire for the possessions of others
10. Tending to delay
12. Manageable; easily handled
16. Ridicule
18. Judgement; wisdom
19. Advanced; chased after
20. To be discontented or in low spirits

Pride & Prejudice Vocabulary Crossword 4

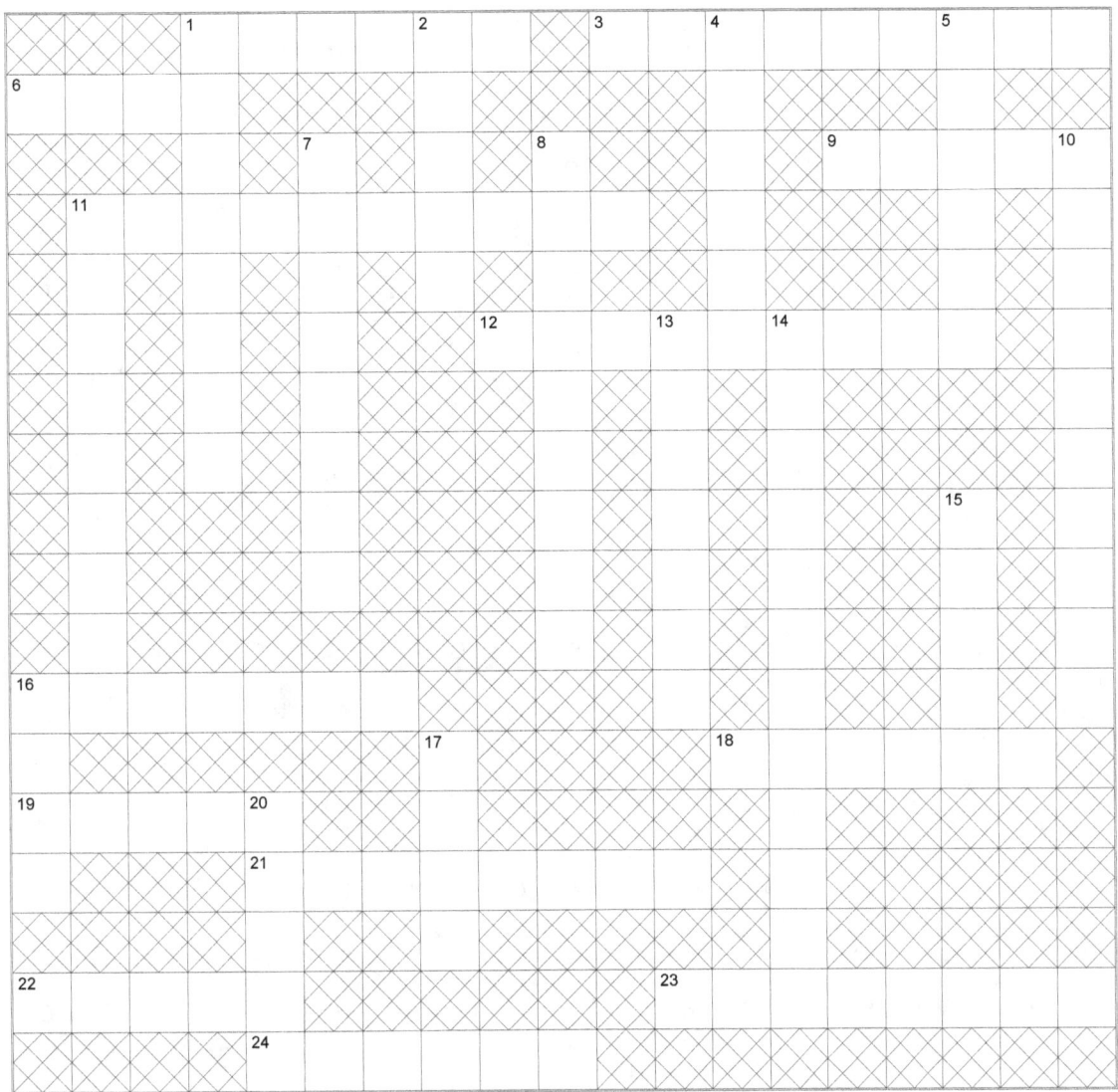

Across
1. Credit
3. Relating to money
6. A sign of the future
9. Thicket of small trees
11. Favorable
12. Manageable; easily handled
16. Intense joy
18. Money given to support the clergy
19. Legal and binding
21. Effectiveness
22. Fashion; popularity
23. Judgement; wisdom
24. To be discontented or in low spirits

Down
1. Insulting; disrespectful; rude
2. Implied by action
4. Convincing
5. Desire; have an ambition or goal
7. Tending to delay
8. Grumbling; complaining
10. Pleas
11. Praise; compliment
13. Impulsive change of mind
14. Finding out; discovering
15. Unclear; not well defined
16. Desire for the possessions of others
17. Empty
20. Postpone

Pride & Prejudice Vocabulary Crossword 4 Answer Key

Across
1. Credit
3. Relating to money
6. A sign of the future
9. Thicket of small trees
11. Favorable
12. Manageable; easily handled
16. Intense joy
18. Money given to support the clergy
19. Legal and binding
21. Effectiveness
22. Fashion; popularity
23. Judgement; wisdom
24. To be discontented or in low spirits

Down
1. Insulting; disrespectful; rude
2. Implied by action
4. Convincing
5. Desire; have an ambition or goal
7. Tending to delay
8. Grumbling; complaining
10. Pleas
11. Praise; compliment
13. Impulsive change of mind
14. Finding out; discovering
15. Unclear; not well defined
16. Desire for the possessions of others
17. Empty
20. Postpone

Pride & Prejudice Vocabulary Juggle Letters 1

1. PNIEER = 1. _____
   To be discontented or in low spirits

2. ERBYITV = 2. _____
   Shortness; quality of being short in duration

3. IMICRETCPUNOCS = 3. _____
   Prudence

4. OLENSITN = 4. _____
   Insulting; disrespectful; rude

5. UOVGE = 5. _____
   Fashion; popularity

6. ARUTICTN = 6. _____
   Not talkative

7. MUAEETDGN = 7. _____
   Added

8. NEIFOUFS = 8. _____
   Unrestrained outpouring of speech

9. ITACT = 9. _____
   Implied by action

10. NCTUINIJSNO = 10. _____
    Commands; orders

11. ICATRNESGAIN = 11. _____
    Finding out; discovering

12. ATGPOEFLIR = 12. _____
    Wasteful; extravagant

13. SFODSTIAUI = 13. _____
    Meticulous; concerned with details; difficult to please

14. UPIOTISRPO = 14. _____
    Favorable

15. YNEV = 15. _____
    Desire for the possessions of others

Pride & Prejudice Vocabulary Juggle Letters 1 Answer Key

1. PNIEER = 1. REPINE
   To be discontented or in low spirits

2. ERBYITV = 2. BREVITY
   Shortness; quality of being short in duration

3. IMICRETCPUNOCS = 3. CIRCUMSPECTION
   Prudence

4. OLENSITN = 4. INSOLENT
   Insulting; disrespectful; rude

5. UOVGE = 5. VOGUE
   Fashion; popularity

6. ARUTICTN = 6. TACITURN
   Not talkative

7. MUAEETDGN = 7. AUGMENTED
   Added

8. NEIFOUFS = 8. EFFUSION
   Unrestrained outpouring of speech

9. ITACT = 9. TACIT
   Implied by action

10. NCTUINIJSNO = 10. INJUNCTIONS
    Commands; orders

11. ICATRNESGAIN = 11. ASCERTAINING
    Finding out; discovering

12. ATGPOEFLIR = 12. PROFLIGATE
    Wasteful; extravagant

13. SFODSTIAUI = 13. FASTIDIOUS
    Meticulous; concerned with details; difficult to please

14. UPIOTISRPO = 14. PROPITIOUS
    Favorable

15. YNEV = 15. ENVY
    Desire for the possessions of others

Pride & Prejudice Vocabulary Juggle Letters 2

1. DETIEURQ = 1. _____
   Repaid

2. RSDOGNSEE = 2. _____
   Totally occupied

3. URPMDECINE = 3. _____
   Characteristic of making unwise decisions

4. ARTTEALBC = 4. _____
   Manageable; easily handled

5. CIIUNOJSNTN = 5. _____
   Commands; orders

6. AOLYDITR = 6. _____
   Tending to delay

7. REPINACGY = 7. _____
   Praise; compliment

8. ITUPEM = 8. _____
   Credit

9. TNUTICRA = 9. _____
   Not talkative

10. TLSENINO = 10. _____
    Insulting; disrespectful; rude

11. DIVO = 11. _____
    Empty

12. ODUFAISSIT = 12. _____
    Meticulous; concerned with details; difficult to please

13. MIAPEBLLCA = 13. _____
    Impossible to appease or please

14. UQELRUSOU = 14. _____
    Grumbling; complaining

15. PRIENE = 15. _____
    To be discontented or in low spirits

Pride & Prejudice Vocabulary Juggle Letters 2 Answer Key

1. DETIEURQ = 1. REQUITED
   Repaid

2. RSDOGNSEE = 2. ENGROSSED
   Totally occupied

3. URPMDECINE = 3. IMPRUDENCE
   Characteristic of making unwise decisions

4. ARTTEALBC = 4. TRACTABLE
   Manageable; easily handled

5. CIIUNOJSNTN = 5. INJUNCTIONS
   Commands; orders

6. AOLYDITR = 6. DILATORY
   Tending to delay

7. REPINACGY = 7. PANEGYRIC
   Praise; compliment

8. ITUPEM = 8. IMPUTE
   Credit

9. TNUTICRA = 9. TACITURN
   Not talkative

10. TLSENINO = 10. INSOLENT
    Insulting; disrespectful; rude

11. DIVO = 11. VOID
    Empty

12. ODUFAISSIT = 12. FASTIDIOUS
    Meticulous; concerned with details; difficult to please

13. MIAPEBLLCA = 13. IMPLACABLE
    Impossible to appease or please

14. UQELRUSOU = 14. QUERULOUS
    Grumbling; complaining

15. PRIENE = 15. REPINE
    To be discontented or in low spirits

Pride & Prejudice Vocabulary Juggle Letters 3

1. DURNPMEECI = 1. _____
   Characteristic of making unwise decisions

2. GEBIOL = 2. _____
   Do a favor or service for

3. IUBIVLLOYT = 3. _____
   Fluency of speech

4. MLCBLAEPAI = 4. _____
   Impossible to appease or please

5. ETTUEISTD = 5. _____
   Lacking; poor

6. USUEOIISRCLP = 6. _____
   Haughty; disdainful

7. LBAFFYIITA = 7. _____
   Quality of being pleasant & easy to speak with

8. ISEPAR = 8. _____
   Desire; have an ambition or goal

9. CETOURNCJE = 9. _____
   Guess

10. NTSIJNINOUC = 10. _____
    Commands; orders

11. RECIAPYUN = 11. _____
    Relating to money

12. FICFEAYC = 12. _____
    Effectiveness

13. NGDERSEOS = 13. _____
    Totally occupied

14. NECVIEVSIT = 14. _____
    Abusive language

15. IATCTNUR = 15. _____
    Not talkative

Pride & Prejudice Vocabulary Juggle Letters 3 Answer Key

1. DURNPMEECI = 1. IMPRUDENCE
   Characteristic of making unwise decisions

2. GEBIOL = 2. OBLIGE
   Do a favor or service for

3. IUBIVLLOYT = 3. VOLUBILITY
   Fluency of speech

4. MLCBLAEPAI = 4. IMPLACABLE
   Impossible to appease or please

5. ETTUEISTD = 5. DESTITUTE
   Lacking; poor

6. USUEOIISRCLP = 6. SUPERCILIOUS
   Haughty; disdainful

7. LBAFFYIITA = 7. AFFABILITY
   Quality of being pleasant & easy to speak with

8. ISEPAR = 8. ASPIRE
   Desire; have an ambition or goal

9. CETOURNCJE = 9. CONJECTURE
   Guess

10. NTSIJNINOUC = 10. INJUNCTIONS
    Commands; orders

11. RECIAPYUN = 11. PECUNIARY
    Relating to money

12. FICFEAYC = 12. EFFICACY
    Effectiveness

13. NGDERSEOS = 13. ENGROSSED
    Totally occupied

14. NECVIEVSIT = 14. INVECTIVES
    Abusive language

15. IATCTNUR = 15. TACITURN
    Not talkative

Pride & Prejudice Vocabulary Juggle Letters 4

1. NEOM = 1. _____
A sign of the future

2. PIACRCE = 2. _____
Impulsive change of mind

3. AUVEG = 3. _____
Unclear; not well defined

4. STUIOOPPIR = 4. _____
Favorable

5. INEITAAGRNSC = 5. _____
Finding out; discovering

6. NUNCBTMEI = 6. _____
Imposed as a duty or obligation

7. OIVD = 7. _____
Empty

8. MPEIUT = 8. _____
Credit

9. EERFD = 9. _____
Postpone

10. ILAOPEFTGR = 10. _____
Wasteful; extravagant

11. ATONSTUOISET = 11. _____
Pretentious; pompous

12. STFSIODAUI = 12. _____
Meticulous; concerned with details; difficult to please

13. EPRSDUU = 13. _____
Advanced; chased after

14. CSIEITNVVE = 14. _____
Abusive language

15. GNRFLIIT = 15. _____
Of little significance

Pride & Prejudice Vocabulary Juggle Letters 4 Answer Key

1. NEOM = 1. OMEN
A sign of the future

2. PIACRCE = 2. CAPRICE
Impulsive change of mind

3. AUVEG = 3. VAGUE
Unclear; not well defined

4. STUIOOPPIR = 4. PROPITIOUS
Favorable

5. INEITAAGRNSC = 5. ASCERTAINING
Finding out; discovering

6. NUNCBTMEI = 6. INCUMBENT
Imposed as a duty or obligation

7. OIVD = 7. VOID
Empty

8. MPEIUT = 8. IMPUTE
Credit

9. EERFD = 9. DEFER
Postpone

10. ILAOPEFTGR =10. PROFLIGATE
Wasteful; extravagant

11. ATONSTUOISET =11. OSTENTATIOUS
Pretentious; pompous

12. STFSIODAUI =12. FASTIDIOUS
Meticulous; concerned with details; difficult to please

13. EPRSDUU =13. PURSUED
Advanced; chased after

14. CSIEITNVVE =14. INVECTIVES
Abusive language

15. GNRFLIIT =15. TRIFLING
Of little significance

AFFABILITY	Quality of being pleasant & easy to speak with
AFFINITY	Natural attraction to
ALACRITY	Cheerful willingness
APPROBATION	Approval
ASCERTAINING	Finding out; discovering
ASPIRE	Desire; have an ambition or goal

AUGMENTED	Added
BREVITY	Shortness; quality of being short in duration
CAPRICE	Impulsive change of mind
CIRCUMSPECTION	Prudence
COGENT	Convincing
CONJECTURE	Guess

CONJUGAL	Relating to marriage
COPSE	Thicket of small trees
DEFER	Postpone
DERISION	Ridicule
DESTITUTE	Lacking; poor
DILATORY	Tending to delay

DIMINUTION	Reduction
ECSTASY	Intense joy
EFFICACY	Effectiveness
EFFUSION	Unrestrained outpouring of speech
ENGROSSED	Totally occupied
ENTREATIES	Pleas

ENVY	Desire for the possessions of others
FASTIDIOUS	Meticulous; concerned with details; difficult to please
IMPERTINENT	Improperly bold or forward
IMPLACABLE	Impossible to appease or please
IMPRUDENCE	Characteristic of making unwise decisions
IMPUTE	Credit

INCUMBENT	Imposed as a duty or obligation
INJUNCTIONS	Commands; orders
INSOLENT	Insulting; disrespectful; rude
INVECTIVES	Abusive language
MERCENARY	Motivated by money or material goods
OBEISANCE	Gesture of deference or homage

OBLIGE	Do a favor or service for
OMEN	A sign of the future
OSTENTATIOUS	Pretentious; pompous
PANEGYRIC	Praise; compliment
PECUNIARY	Relating to money
PERPETUALLY	Continually; constantly

PLIANCY	Flexibility
PROFLIGATE	Wasteful; extravagant
PROPITIOUS	Favorable
PURSUED	Advanced; chased after
QUERULOUS	Grumbling; complaining
RECTITUDE	Moral uprightness

REPINE	To be discontented or in low spirits
REQUITED	Repaid
SAGACITY	Judgement; wisdom
SANGUINE	Cheerfully confident; optimistic
SCRUPLE	Hesitate as a result of conscience
SUPERCILIOUS	Haughty; disdainful

TACIT	Implied by action
TACITURN	Not talkative
TITHES	Money given to support the clergy
TRACTABLE	Manageable; easily handled
TRIFLING	Of little significance
VAGUE	Unclear; not well defined

VALID	Legal and binding
VERACITY	Truthfulness
VOGUE	Fashion; popularity
VOID	Empty
VOLUBILITY	Fluency of speech

Pride & Prejudice Vocabulary

SAGACITY	TACIT	INCUMBENT	REPINE	PANEGYRIC
ASCERTAINING	CAPRICE	AUGMENTED	DEFER	ENGROSSED
IMPUTE	EFFICACY	FREE SPACE	DERISION	COPSE
REQUITED	IMPERTINENT	EFFUSION	PECUNIARY	OBLIGE
CONJECTURE	ENVY	VOGUE	CONJUGAL	SANGUINE

Pride & Prejudice Vocabulary

OSTENTATIOUS	ASPIRE	IMPRUDENCE	PROPITIOUS	INSOLENT
PLIANCY	ECSTASY	VOID	QUERULOUS	FASTIDIOUS
DILATORY	INVECTIVES	FREE SPACE	DIMINUTION	TRACTABLE
PROFLIGATE	MERCENARY	VOLUBILITY	COGENT	TITHES
INJUNCTIONS	BREVITY	APPROBATION	OBEISANCE	VAGUE

Pride & Prejudice Vocabulary

IMPLACABLE	PROPITIOUS	PECUNIARY	IMPERTINENT	ENTREATIES
APPROBATION	SCRUPLE	REPINE	CAPRICE	AFFINITY
INVECTIVES	AUGMENTED	FREE SPACE	COGENT	VAGUE
VOGUE	BREVITY	ENVY	DERISION	SANGUINE
CONJUGAL	VOID	COPSE	TRACTABLE	PURSUED

Pride & Prejudice Vocabulary

FASTIDIOUS	VERACITY	INSOLENT	QUERULOUS	SUPERCILIOUS
EFFUSION	INJUNCTIONS	EFFICACY	MERCENARY	DIMINUTION
DILATORY	VOLUBILITY	FREE SPACE	TACIT	ENGROSSED
CIRCUMSPECTION	PERPETUALLY	OSTENTATIOUS	RECTITUDE	PROFLIGATE
OBEISANCE	IMPRUDENCE	DESTITUTE	PANEGYRIC	SAGACITY

Pride & Prejudice Vocabulary

DIMINUTION	IMPLACABLE	PLIANCY	ENVY	OSTENTATIOUS
ASPIRE	COPSE	OBEISANCE	IMPERTINENT	SUPERCILIOUS
VOGUE	PURSUED	FREE SPACE	PROFLIGATE	VERACITY
IMPUTE	ASCERTAINING	REQUITED	QUERULOUS	APPROBATION
PECUNIARY	TACIT	CIRCUMSPECTION	PROPITIOUS	SANGUINE

Pride & Prejudice Vocabulary

DERISION	VAGUE	OMEN	ECSTASY	PANEGYRIC
INJUNCTIONS	DILATORY	CONJECTURE	ALACRITY	REPINE
RECTITUDE	TACITURN	FREE SPACE	CONJUGAL	TRIFLING
INSOLENT	TRACTABLE	BREVITY	INVECTIVES	SAGACITY
VOLUBILITY	CAPRICE	OBLIGE	COGENT	IMPRUDENCE

Pride & Prejudice Vocabulary

TRACTABLE	RECTITUDE	PURSUED	CIRCUMSPECTION	ECSTASY
INSOLENT	VOLUBILITY	ENTREATIES	CONJUGAL	ENVY
VOGUE	PROPITIOUS	FREE SPACE	PLIANCY	INVECTIVES
TACITURN	SAGACITY	CAPRICE	BREVITY	IMPRUDENCE
ALACRITY	PROFLIGATE	DIMINUTION	PANEGYRIC	VOID

Pride & Prejudice Vocabulary

MERCENARY	EFFUSION	REQUITED	AUGMENTED	ENGROSSED
ASCERTAINING	VERACITY	SANGUINE	INCUMBENT	OSTENTATIOUS
DILATORY	AFFABILITY	FREE SPACE	INJUNCTIONS	APPROBATION
TRIFLING	SUPERCILIOUS	QUERULOUS	VALID	PECUNIARY
TITHES	SCRUPLE	DERISION	IMPERTINENT	COPSE

Pride & Prejudice Vocabulary

VAGUE	DILATORY	VERACITY	AUGMENTED	OBLIGE
VOID	SAGACITY	PERPETUALLY	SCRUPLE	SANGUINE
CIRCUMSPECTION	TRIFLING	FREE SPACE	PROFLIGATE	PURSUED
DESTITUTE	VALID	MERCENARY	APPROBATION	DEFER
PECUNIARY	INCUMBENT	IMPLACABLE	RECTITUDE	INVECTIVES

Pride & Prejudice Vocabulary

TACIT	SUPERCILIOUS	INSOLENT	REQUITED	OSTENTATIOUS
OBEISANCE	CONJUGAL	ECSTASY	PLIANCY	EFFUSION
CAPRICE	INJUNCTIONS	FREE SPACE	ENTREATIES	ASPIRE
ENVY	IMPUTE	BREVITY	ALACRITY	DIMINUTION
IMPERTINENT	QUERULOUS	DERISION	FASTIDIOUS	AFFABILITY

Pride & Prejudice Vocabulary

PECUNIARY	SUPERCILIOUS	VOID	PROFLIGATE	DIMINUTION
OBLIGE	IMPUTE	CIRCUMSPECTION	TITHES	VAGUE
DILATORY	SANGUINE	FREE SPACE	REQUITED	VERACITY
INVECTIVES	INSOLENT	ENGROSSED	PERPETUALLY	VOGUE
IMPRUDENCE	AFFINITY	ALACRITY	ECSTASY	MERCENARY

Pride & Prejudice Vocabulary

VALID	APPROBATION	TACIT	TRIFLING	DERISION
ENVY	RECTITUDE	PROPITIOUS	ENTREATIES	PANEGYRIC
EFFICACY	COGENT	FREE SPACE	REPINE	AUGMENTED
COPSE	SCRUPLE	PURSUED	DEFER	TACITURN
AFFABILITY	PLIANCY	FASTIDIOUS	ASPIRE	ASCERTAINING

Pride & Prejudice Vocabulary

TACITURN	SUPERCILIOUS	CAPRICE	SAGACITY	ECSTASY
EFFICACY	VOLUBILITY	CONJECTURE	ENVY	OBEISANCE
PERPETUALLY	TITHES	FREE SPACE	COGENT	DEFER
TRACTABLE	ASCERTAINING	VOID	VALID	EFFUSION
QUERULOUS	IMPERTINENT	CONJUGAL	VERACITY	SANGUINE

Pride & Prejudice Vocabulary

PECUNIARY	INJUNCTIONS	INSOLENT	PROFLIGATE	OMEN
PANEGYRIC	RECTITUDE	IMPRUDENCE	INCUMBENT	OBLIGE
ASPIRE	AFFINITY	FREE SPACE	BREVITY	AUGMENTED
APPROBATION	COPSE	REPINE	VAGUE	TACIT
FASTIDIOUS	REQUITED	DILATORY	IMPLACABLE	DERISION

Pride & Prejudice Vocabulary

ALACRITY	OMEN	CONJECTURE	AFFABILITY	DIMINUTION
INJUNCTIONS	BREVITY	TITHES	ENTREATIES	PECUNIARY
SCRUPLE	FASTIDIOUS	FREE SPACE	SUPERCILIOUS	TRACTABLE
ASPIRE	CONJUGAL	AUGMENTED	INCUMBENT	REPINE
INSOLENT	CIRCUMSPECTION	IMPRUDENCE	PERPETUALLY	RECTITUDE

Pride & Prejudice Vocabulary

COPSE	DEFER	VALID	MERCENARY	COGENT
VAGUE	SANGUINE	IMPUTE	OBEISANCE	SAGACITY
DERISION	PROPITIOUS	FREE SPACE	PURSUED	EFFICACY
OSTENTATIOUS	IMPERTINENT	APPROBATION	IMPLACABLE	ENVY
VOGUE	PROFLIGATE	VOLUBILITY	VOID	ECSTASY

Pride & Prejudice Vocabulary

INCUMBENT	SAGACITY	ASPIRE	EFFICACY	CONJECTURE
OBEISANCE	VOID	IMPRUDENCE	AUGMENTED	IMPERTINENT
INVECTIVES	PROFLIGATE	FREE SPACE	VOLUBILITY	INJUNCTIONS
ASCERTAINING	COPSE	OBLIGE	SCRUPLE	FASTIDIOUS
APPROBATION	VERACITY	DEFER	VALID	SUPERCILIOUS

Pride & Prejudice Vocabulary

REPINE	DESTITUTE	DILATORY	MERCENARY	CONJUGAL
EFFUSION	BREVITY	PURSUED	IMPLACABLE	ECSTASY
QUERULOUS	AFFABILITY	FREE SPACE	DIMINUTION	VOGUE
AFFINITY	ENVY	REQUITED	PROPITIOUS	TITHES
ENTREATIES	VAGUE	TACIT	COGENT	DERISION

Pride & Prejudice Vocabulary

APPROBATION	INJUNCTIONS	VOID	PURSUED	VOGUE
INSOLENT	INVECTIVES	PROFLIGATE	IMPERTINENT	PLIANCY
TRACTABLE	TRIFLING	FREE SPACE	PECUNIARY	QUERULOUS
DILATORY	ENGROSSED	OBEISANCE	SUPERCILIOUS	ENTREATIES
PROPITIOUS	TACITURN	IMPRUDENCE	ENVY	RECTITUDE

Pride & Prejudice Vocabulary

CONJUGAL	VALID	ALACRITY	AFFINITY	MERCENARY
BREVITY	PANEGYRIC	VOLUBILITY	DIMINUTION	TITHES
AUGMENTED	FASTIDIOUS	FREE SPACE	COGENT	DESTITUTE
OSTENTATIOUS	INCUMBENT	OMEN	REPINE	ASPIRE
VERACITY	CAPRICE	EFFICACY	PERPETUALLY	ASCERTAINING

Pride & Prejudice Vocabulary

OBLIGE	OMEN	VOLUBILITY	VOGUE	EFFICACY
TRIFLING	INCUMBENT	IMPUTE	ENTREATIES	DEFER
RECTITUDE	CONJECTURE	FREE SPACE	ALACRITY	APPROBATION
PURSUED	PLIANCY	DERISION	AFFABILITY	INVECTIVES
SANGUINE	VERACITY	DILATORY	TRACTABLE	PERPETUALLY

Pride & Prejudice Vocabulary

EFFUSION	PECUNIARY	TACITURN	PROFLIGATE	VAGUE
VOID	ASCERTAINING	MERCENARY	COGENT	IMPRUDENCE
ENVY	VALID	FREE SPACE	SUPERCILIOUS	ENGROSSED
IMPERTINENT	BREVITY	REQUITED	PROPITIOUS	AFFINITY
ASPIRE	CIRCUMSPECTION	SCRUPLE	REPINE	ECSTASY

Pride & Prejudice Vocabulary

INCUMBENT	VALID	PURSUED	VERACITY	SANGUINE
COGENT	AUGMENTED	OSTENTATIOUS	APPROBATION	QUERULOUS
VOLUBILITY	EFFICACY	FREE SPACE	ASCERTAINING	ENVY
ALACRITY	AFFABILITY	FASTIDIOUS	PROFLIGATE	REPINE
CONJECTURE	VAGUE	DEFER	IMPLACABLE	TRIFLING

Pride & Prejudice Vocabulary

ENGROSSED	PANEGYRIC	PECUNIARY	COPSE	ASPIRE
TACITURN	MERCENARY	SCRUPLE	ECSTASY	TACIT
IMPERTINENT	INJUNCTIONS	FREE SPACE	RECTITUDE	VOGUE
VOID	OMEN	REQUITED	IMPUTE	DIMINUTION
DILATORY	SAGACITY	DESTITUTE	INSOLENT	CONJUGAL

Pride & Prejudice Vocabulary

REPINE	DIMINUTION	AFFINITY	BREVITY	OBEISANCE
OSTENTATIOUS	PLIANCY	ENVY	ASCERTAINING	INJUNCTIONS
REQUITED	FASTIDIOUS	FREE SPACE	VERACITY	TACITURN
ENTREATIES	COGENT	INCUMBENT	SANGUINE	PROFLIGATE
IMPERTINENT	INVECTIVES	TACIT	VOID	ECSTASY

Pride & Prejudice Vocabulary

INSOLENT	TRIFLING	QUERULOUS	RECTITUDE	VAGUE
DILATORY	CONJUGAL	PECUNIARY	IMPUTE	PURSUED
SUPERCILIOUS	PANEGYRIC	FREE SPACE	DEFER	CONJECTURE
ENGROSSED	PERPETUALLY	AUGMENTED	SCRUPLE	VOGUE
OBLIGE	AFFABILITY	TITHES	VOLUBILITY	VALID

Pride & Prejudice Vocabulary

ENVY	PROPITIOUS	SAGACITY	ASCERTAINING	SUPERCILIOUS
FASTIDIOUS	ENTREATIES	TACIT	OSTENTATIOUS	ECSTASY
PERPETUALLY	QUERULOUS	FREE SPACE	EFFICACY	INVECTIVES
ALACRITY	INSOLENT	VERACITY	AUGMENTED	INCUMBENT
SANGUINE	VOLUBILITY	REPINE	IMPLACABLE	IMPERTINENT

Pride & Prejudice Vocabulary

CONJUGAL	ENGROSSED	EFFUSION	PLIANCY	IMPRUDENCE
TRIFLING	APPROBATION	RECTITUDE	SCRUPLE	INJUNCTIONS
TITHES	OMEN	FREE SPACE	VOID	DILATORY
COPSE	AFFINITY	AFFABILITY	DERISION	CIRCUMSPECTION
IMPUTE	TACITURN	VOGUE	TRACTABLE	VAGUE

Pride & Prejudice Vocabulary

CONJECTURE	INSOLENT	VERACITY	CIRCUMSPECTION	MERCENARY
PURSUED	APPROBATION	OMEN	CONJUGAL	AFFINITY
TACIT	TRIFLING	FREE SPACE	BREVITY	OBEISANCE
REPINE	ECSTASY	INJUNCTIONS	PLIANCY	OSTENTATIOUS
ALACRITY	ASCERTAINING	FASTIDIOUS	QUERULOUS	IMPRUDENCE

Pride & Prejudice Vocabulary

ENGROSSED	TITHES	SANGUINE	REQUITED	AUGMENTED
COGENT	ENVY	VAGUE	EFFUSION	VOLUBILITY
IMPUTE	CAPRICE	FREE SPACE	PROFLIGATE	OBLIGE
DIMINUTION	PROPITIOUS	SAGACITY	VALID	DESTITUTE
RECTITUDE	IMPERTINENT	PECUNIARY	PANEGYRIC	TACITURN

Pride & Prejudice Vocabulary

COGENT	CONJUGAL	VOLUBILITY	INCUMBENT	IMPLACABLE
TACIT	TRACTABLE	DERISION	CAPRICE	OBLIGE
PURSUED	ENVY	FREE SPACE	OMEN	QUERULOUS
DILATORY	VOGUE	ENTREATIES	SCRUPLE	COPSE
PLIANCY	CONJECTURE	IMPERTINENT	INJUNCTIONS	SANGUINE

Pride & Prejudice Vocabulary

PECUNIARY	BREVITY	APPROBATION	VOID	OSTENTATIOUS
CIRCUMSPECTION	IMPUTE	SAGACITY	PROFLIGATE	SUPERCILIOUS
TACITURN	ASCERTAINING	FREE SPACE	DESTITUTE	EFFICACY
ALACRITY	MERCENARY	FASTIDIOUS	VERACITY	TITHES
PANEGYRIC	VAGUE	DIMINUTION	PROPITIOUS	AUGMENTED